MW00989868

THE SMELL OF

SAWDUST

What Evangelicals
Can Learn from Their
Fundamentalist Heritage

THE SMELL OF
SAWDUST

RICHARD J. MOUW

ZondervanPublishingHouse
Grand Rapids, Michigan

The Smell of Sawdust
Copyright © 2000 by Richard J. Mouw

Requests for information should be addressed to:

🏭 ZondervanPublishingHouse
Grand Rapids, Michigan 49530

Library of Congress Cataloging-in-Publication Data
Mouw, Richard J.
    The smell of sawdust: what evangelicals can learn from their fundamentalist
heritage / Richard J. Mouw.
       p. cm.
    Includes bibliographical references.
    ISBN: 0-310-23196-5
    1. Evangelism. 2. Fundamentalism. 3. Mouw, Richard J. I. Title.
BF1640 .M68 2000
270.8'2--dc21

                                00-042877

This edition is printed on acid-free paper.

All Scripture quotations, unless otherwise indicated, are taken from the *Holy Bible: New International Version*®. NIV®. Copyright © 1973, 1978, 1984 by International Bible Society. Used by permission of Zondervan Publishing House. All rights reserved.

All rights reserved. No part of this publication may be reproduced, stored in a retrieval system, or transmitted in any form or by any means—electronic, mechanical, photocopy, recording, or any other—except for brief quotations in printed reviews, without the prior permission of the publisher.

Interior design by Rob Monacelli

Printed in the United States of America

---

00 01 02 03 04 05 /❖ DC/ 10 9 8 7 6 5 4 3 2 1

CONTENTS

CHAPTER ONE

OF TENTS AND TRAILS

Acclaimed author Annie Dillard tells the story of a time in her childhood when she and her sister attended a Presbyterian church camp. "If our parents had known how pious and low-church this camp was," she said, "they would have yanked us." This was a place where children memorized passages from the Bible, sang lively gospel songs, and gathered for informal prayer meetings. And here's my favorite line: "The faith-filled theology there was only half a step out of a tent; you could still smell the sawdust."[1]

In mentioning sawdust, she was referring, of course, to the old "gospel tent meetings," where traveling evangelists and revival preachers held forth. Under those canopies—where a layer of sawdust was often spread on the ground—sinners were urged to walk "the sawdust trail" to the front of the meeting place, where they could kneel and repent of their sins.

I attended tent meetings in my youth, and I remember the sawdust, along with many other sights and sounds of those services. The memories are pleasant ones. I cannot recall ever being bored at a tent meeting. The music lives on in my soul, as do many of the phrases and stories of the sermons I heard. I know some people—a few of them are good friends—who would love to erase these memories altogether. Not me. I can still smell the sawdust, and this aroma carries with it spiritual associations that have shaped my understanding of what it means to be a Christian human being. And I think it is important—not only for myself but for the evangelical movement in general—to keep smelling the sawdust.

In the following pages I will reflect on the strengths of the sawdust trail legacy. I will also speak honestly about some of its weaknesses. I have spent a good part of my life thus far working with other evangelicals who have been dedicated to correcting some of the defects and excesses associated with the religion of the sawdust trail. This has been time well spent. But I've also begun to worry lately that in our criticisms we have lost sight of some of the good things. I'm convinced it is healthy for the evangelical movement to keep smelling the sawdust.

Needless to say, those strengths were not dependent on actual sawdust. I will use the image of the sawdust trail both in its literal sense and as a symbol for a larger assortment of similar evangelical gatherings: "gospel tabernacles," summer Bible conferences, camp meetings, and early evangelistic radio broadcasts. And while my own experience of the sawdust trail took place largely within the confines of the fundamentalist movement, I also will have in mind here the ways in which Holiness and Pentecostal Christians also thrived on the smell of sawdust. Nor will I forget the fact that the sawdust trail was itself a continuation of earlier pathways, such as those blazed by people who made their way out of the European cathedrals into intimate house church fellowships, by circuit riders, and by plantation slaves who walked—and ran— the difficult path to freedom.

Finding Home

I have long assumed that the main reason for the sawdust in the revival tents was to keep things from getting too muddy—and it surely did serve this function. But recently I discovered that the image of a sawdust trail also had an important metaphorical meaning, derived from the nineteenth-century lumber camps. When lumberjacks got lost in the woods, they would walk in various directions until they found sawdust on the ground. Then they would follow the sawdust trail back to a place of safety. The evangelist Billy Sunday knew of this practice, and he used the image in calling sinners to follow the sawdust trail to a place of spiritual safety.

Finding the way home has long been an important evangelical theme. It's also an image that speaks to my own soul. A Roman Catholic theologian recently invited me to write a few paragraphs about how I understand what it means to "know God"; these thoughts would be included in a book of reflections by people from various religious traditions. I began my contribution by quoting a bumper sticker I had seen a few years ago. I usually don't get much good theology from reading the short messages I encounter on California freeways, but this one struck me as quite profound: "You are a child of God. Please call home." This is as good an answer as any I can imagine of what it means to find God. The "home" image expresses a basic motif in the biblical portrayal of our human quest for spiritual fulfillment.

In an essay published over a half-century ago, German philosopher Martin Heidegger predicted that "homelessness is coming to be the destiny of the world."[2] Heidegger wasn't thinking so much of the literal homelessness we see so much of in our cities today. Rather, he was prophesying about a growing sense of aimlessness in human life—the loss of a sense of belonging that is so much a part of what is referred to these days as the "postmodern" experience.

Heidegger's prophecy was an accurate one. And we can hear strong voices today actually praising this experience of homelessness. A well-known psychologist wrote a book a while back in which he argued that the best way to help folks who are living aimless lives is to provide them with the coping skills necessary for the exciting journey of an "endless wandering in the maze of meaning."[3] He summarized his approach by quoting a phrase coined by another scholar: *mazing grace.* Those of us who can still smell the sawdust refuse to drop the letter "a" from this phrase. To be sure, we also know what it is like to wander. Our own lives have taken us "through many dangers, toils, and snares." But our pilgrimages are not aimless ones: "'Tis grace hath brought [us] safe thus far, and grace will lead [us] home." We have found the path that leads us to a place of eternal safety.

Songs of the Trail

A group of evangelical scholars were invited to Harvard Divinity School in January of 1998 to give a presentation on the strengths and weaknesses of contemporary evangelicalism. For me the highlight was a lecture by Mark Noll of Wheaton College. As he talked about "Evangelicalism at its Best," he developed the idea that we evangelicals are at our best when we are singing our hymns. Evangelical theology comes to life in the songs we sing.

I heartily agree. Hymns have certainly been a shaping influence in my spiritual life. A friend who knows me well tells people, "When Mouw gets backed into a corner, he quotes a hymn!" He's right. I like to quote hymns to make a point. And I will give free rein to this habit in this book.

But not just for nostalgia's sake. The old hymns have taken on new meanings for me as I've struggled with my evangelical identity. Here is one special example. There was a time a few decades ago when I began thinking a lot about our need to reach out to the poor and the oppressed. This wasn't something I heard much about in the sermons and Bible lessons of my childhood and youth. But it became clear to me that the Bible regularly urges us to take up the cause of those who are needy. Furthermore, it struck me that the biblical writers—Amos and James, for example— weren't just talking about charity; they were addressing *systems and structures* of injustice.

One night I gave a speech on this subject to a Christian gathering, and a man in the audience became quite upset about what I was saying. He challenged me angrily: "You didn't learn that stuff from the Bible—you got it from Karl Marx!" As I thought about how to respond, suddenly some lines from a gospel hymn came to mind. I told him that when I was a kid, our family bought a new record player—my first one, the windup kind—and I was given a collection of hymns sung by George Beverly Shea. I was so fascinated with my new technology that I played the record over and over, and in the process I memorized all of the hymns on it. So when the man in the audience accused me of being a Marxist, I quoted one of those hymns in response:

> *I'd rather have Jesus than silver or gold,*
> *I'd rather have Him than riches untold;*
> *I'd rather have Jesus than houses or lands,*
> *I'd rather be true to His nail-pierced hands.*

And I said, "Once you've learned your lessons in economics from the songs of George Beverly Shea, Karl Marx comes off as pretty tame!"

This wasn't just a pleasant piece of rhetoric. The hymns of the sawdust trail contain profound messages about what it means to belong to Jesus, even though the implications of those songs were not always recognized by the people who taught us to sing them.

A student once stopped in to talk to me about problems he was having with his parents. He wanted to devote his life to working with young people in the inner city—but his family strongly disapproved. "When the argument gets really heated," he said, "they start saying racist things about how bad the 'colored people' are." Then the student's eyes filled with tears. "Don't they realize that I'm just following through on things I learned from them? It was my parents who taught me to sing, 'Red and yellow, black and white, they are precious in his sight.' I'm just trying to take seriously what *they* taught me!"

Exploring Implications

The songs and sermons of the sawdust trail told a story of how we human beings, originally created for fellowship with the living God, have lost our way because of our rebelliousness. We chose to disobey our Maker and set out on a futile attempt to chart our own routes to peace and security. But the only way to find the path that can lead us home again is to accept God's gracious offer of salvation through Jesus Christ. Here is how a sawdust song puts it:

> I've wandered far away from God . . .
> The paths of sin too long I've trod . . .
> Open now Thine arms of love—Lord, I'm coming home.

There are themes here I consider nonnegotiable. We are indeed sinners who, when left to our own devises and designs, are hopelessly lost. All we can do is to plead the mercies of the God against whom we have rebelled. There are not many ways home: All paths to God must find their way to the cross of Jesus. The smell of sawdust provides for me a vivid reminder of these very important truths.

But the songs of the sawdust trail also imply a richer message than the one regularly proclaimed in those environs. When I came to a point in my life where I sensed the need to address bigger and more complex questions than the ones I had heard about on the sawdust trail—questions about justice and peace and social righteousness and faith's implications for a life of learning—I found myself not so much rejecting the message of the sawdust trail but rather thinking about the clues it gave me for the broader path of discipleship. I was aware of navigating my way through a larger world of complex questions—but I have always been grateful for the guidance that came with the smell of sawdust in my own life.

CHAPTER TWO

NATURAL SPIRITUALITY

A man wrote to me recently to share some thoughts about his spiritual journey. His roots are fundamentalist, and he still considers himself a strong evangelical. But he has also learned much about the spiritual life in recent years from Roman Catholicism and other "catholic" traditions. He now affirms, he says, that all of these are "living streams" that flow from Jesus himself.

I agree. I'm pleased about the ways in which so many Christians these days are exploring diverse spiritual traditions. As I write these words, my copies of books about the Desert Fathers and "centering prayer" are within my reach. I have received spiritual wisdom in recent years from the Rule of Saint Benedict and the writings of Henri Nouwen, among others. One of my favorite spiritual books—I highly recommend it—is *The Story of a Soul*, by Saint Therese of Lisieux.

But I must also confess that I'm not very good at the kinds of spiritual exercises such writers recommend. If I were given a written test on the contents of Richard Foster's *Celebration of Discipline*, I'm sure I would pass with flying colors; but if the truth is to be known, I often get hung up on a very practical level at that point where I'm supposed to begin twenty minutes of repeating "the Jesus Prayer" by assuming a comfortable posture and finding a relaxed rhythm of breathing.

And I've decided not to feel guilty about this kind of awkwardness. When it comes to spirituality, I think it is important to give serious attention to what comes naturally. Of course, the word "natural" has different meanings. I am "naturally" a sinner—which means that many of my natural impulses do not fit very well into a pattern of holy living. But I have also decided that the "natural" inclinations rooted in my biography and temperament must also be respected.

Providential Preparation

Two recent discoveries have led me to put forth my *do-what-comes-naturally* proposal with some degree of spiritual confidence. The first is a book by Chester P. Michael and Marie C. Norrisey titled *Prayer and Temperament: Different Prayer Forms for Different Personality Types.*[1] The authors sort out several strands of spirituality—especially Benedictine, Ignatian, Augustinian, Franciscan, and Thomistic—and relate them to different Myers-Briggs personality types. I found their discussion illuminating, and it helped me to understand how certain forms of prayer come more easily to me than others.

The second discovery was actually a *rediscovery*. For my spiritual nourishment I regularly go back to Abraham Kuyper's meditations in *To Be Near Unto God;* recently I reread his reflections on the psalmist's declaration that the Lord "didst make me hope when I was upon my mother's breasts" (Psalm 22:9 King James Version). The theme being sounded in this passage, Kuyper insists, is found elsewhere in the Scriptures: that "to form a right estimate of the beginning and the development of our hidden walk with God, we should go back not merely to our conversion, but back of our conversion to our conception and birth." God has been at work with us from the very beginning, shaping us spiritually and psychologically. "As concerns the unique character of our disposition of soul, our gifts and talents, our form of existence, and even of our body, there is here no accident at play, no caprice, no fate, but the counsel and the working of our God." This tells us much, Kuyper says, about how each of us is to find the proper patterns of our unique ways of relating to God. To be sure, we can learn much from our "reading of what certain great spirits have written about their nearness to God." But it is also important to recognize the highly individualized ways in which each of us has been providentially prepared for our hidden walk with the Lord. "This sets you free," writes Kuyper, "from people, even from godly people, who press *their* piety upon you, but you are bound thereby to your God, personally, in everything, from your conception and birth."[2]

For me to suggest that we do what comes naturally, then, is to propose—in good Calvinist fashion—that we do what comes *providentially* to us as persons who have been formed from our earliest days for a life of nearness to God. With this in mind, it can be helpful to set aside Saint Therese and the Desert Fathers for a brief time and think about the "natural" ways in which we sense something of the divine closeness. For example, I regularly sing hymns in the car as I drive to work in the morning. A line like "O to grace how great a debtor / Daily I'm constrained to be!" can touch me in the deep and hidden places of my being.

I haven't read anything in the recent spirituality literature about singing hymns in the car. But I will trust that God has been long at work in me, shaping me into the Myers-Briggs type that I am, so that I may find my own hidden walk with the One who created me.

On the Road

To be sure, I cannot ignore other signs of God's leading. Once when I visited a Benedictine monastery I experienced a profound sense of awe and joy as I witnessed three young monks—in a service where they were taking their final monastic vows—lying prostrate before their abbot. This too is a providential prompting. Our hearts are restless until they rest in God, and the yearning for very new ways of experiencing God's presence can also be a very "natural" leading of the Spirit. God is not done shaping us as we are led into new stages of the hidden walk.

But Abraham Kuyper and the Myers-Briggs people have together convinced me that I do not need to feel guilty when I feel awkward in spiritual exercises that seem to come more naturally to other people. And so with all the spiritual confidence I can muster, I will continue on a regular basis to find a comfortable position behind the steering wheel in the morning, and after finding the appropriate breathing rhythm, I will sing hymns all the way to the office.

CHAPTER THREE

A LABEL WORTH WEARING

T̲ell me, how does a person like you manage to survive in the evangelical world?" My questioner was a minister who had just heard me give a speech at a conference sponsored by an ecumenical group. I had been invited as the token evangelical on the program, and this person wanted to tell me he had been caught off guard by what I had said. He had a bias against evangelicals, he confessed, but he actually liked some of the points I had made. And what he didn't like he still found quite sensible.

Here's how I responded to his question about surviving in the world of evangelicalism: "One thing that helps is that I *really am* an evangelical." I wasn't being flippant. Being an evangelical isn't something I simply endure. I am actually quite enthusiastic about wearing the label. "Surviving" in the evangelical camp isn't something I worry about.

Not that I don't worry about evangelical defects. I think about them a lot. But I fret about them *as* an evangelical. My first impulse is to look within the evangelical tradition as I search for clues about how to correct the defects.

Before going any further, though, I must say something about the "evangelical" label itself. Labels can outlive their usefulness, and it's important to keep monitoring the identification tags we wear to see whether they still make sense. A good label will inform. If a term we use to describe ourselves ceases to live up to the standards of truth-in-advertising, we should drop it.

I have nonevangelical friends who complain about the fact that we have taken ownership of the term. "'Evangelical' has a long history," they say. "In Germany, for example, it is roughly synonymous with 'Protestant.' Why should you folks act like you're the only ones who can describe yourselves in that way?"

I respond by saying that this is the way it goes with labels. Take the denomination called the Disciples of Christ. Don't I have the right to call myself one of Christ's disciples? And the same goes for *catholic* (meaning "universal"), *adventist* (meaning that you believe Jesus Christ will return someday), and *orthodox* (meaning that you are in favor of having the right beliefs). Some Christian labels serve at least two functions: They point to a characteristic widely shared among believers of various stripes — but they also are used to single out a subgroup of the larger Christian community.

In the broader meaning, to be an evangelical is simply to embrace the *evangel*, the gospel. In this sense it is hard to think of any Christian who would not want to admit to having an evangelical faith. But the label also singles out a specific Christian subgroup. Recognizing, then, that every Christian has a right to the evangelical label in its broadest application, *evangelical* is still a label that has come to be identified with a specific group of Christians. And as long as that movement has a discernible identity, the label will continue to be an informative one.

Experiential Christianity

What, then, is the subgroup to which the label applies in this more limited sense? There are different ways to spell it out, but here is my own way of putting it. The evangelical movement is a loose coalition of groups and ministries that have their origins in various branches of Protestant pietism and pietist-type groups. *Pietism* is a pattern of Christianity that has emphasized the experiential dimensions of the Christian faith. European pietism had its beginnings in a reaction against a highly intellectualized orthodoxy that had become the norm in many Lutheran and Reformed churches in the century or so after the Reformation. Early pietist groups protested what they saw as the intellectualistic excesses of rationalistic orthodoxy, whose fascination with "head knowledge"— to use a favorite pietist way of putting things—seemed to be crowding out "heart knowledge."

Today's evangelical movement includes some groups whose histories can be directly traced back to these reactions, as well as other groups—Wesleyans, Pentecostals, Baptists, the heirs of the Puritans, and others—who emphasize experiential motifs similar to those emphasized by the pietists. We present-day evangelicals, like the pietists of the past, insist that to be a Christian, properly understood, is to experience the regeneration of the inner self, so that the claims of the gospel are appropriated in a very personal way. We want people to know Jesus as a living Savior. The Bible for us is a book that God uses in order to speak to each of us about how we should live our lives.

To be sure, we also pay close attention to doctrinal formulations. We care about the way people speak theologically about the authority of Scripture, the Virgin Birth, the atoning work of Christ, and the like. We know that, while concern about doctrine can harden into a rigid dogmatism, it can also serve the critical function of undergirding a warm piety. If the Christian faith rests in a fundamental way on a heartfelt trust in a Savior, then how we understand the person and work of this Savior—and the authority of the Book that instructs us regarding his redemptive program—is a matter of profound importance. Without paying serious attention to what we believe, our experience can, and usually does, lead us in some strange directions.

Church and Parachurch

All of this has implications for the way we evangelicals structure our church life. Two themes stand out in this regard: our strong emphasis on the local fellowship of Christians and our passion for communicating the gospel to the unsaved. These items are understandable, given our pietist heritage. When we have engaged in ecclesiastical battles, we have typically been motivated by concerns that relate directly to the vitality of both the local church and the church's global mission, issues such as who gets to train our pastors and who gets to give direction to the missionary-evangelistic enterprise.

Evangelicals rely heavily on what are often called "parachurch" organizations—groups and ministries that carry on their work at one step removed from the "institutional" church. This too has a long history. In the seventeenth century the pietists typically formed "house churches," or "conventicles," where they met for small group Bible study, prayer, and conversations about Christian living. For some of the pietists, these fellowships were maintained as an add-on to the corporate worship of the official churches. For others they functioned as a substitute for more formal church worship—although many of them evolved into separate churches and denominations.

A few years ago an influential businessman told me about his attempts to find spiritual enrichment. He and his wife belonged to a congregation of a mainline denomination. They weren't unhappy in their local church—both of them were involved in many congregational activities. But he wanted to probe deeper into spiritual matters. He went on "silent retreats" at a nearby monastery, but that experience didn't do much for him. He took some theology courses at a local seminary; he found it interesting, but it wasn't the spiritual nurture he was looking for either. Then a friend invited him to join a half-dozen other business folks who met one morning a week for breakfast and Bible study. "This has changed my life," he told me. "We come from different church backgrounds, but we have a common desire to understand what the Bible means for our daily lives. I'm still very involved in church—but that breakfast time is where it really happens for me!"

This man found a source of spiritual nurture that is very typical in the pietist tradition. He discovered like-minded Christians, all of whom also were involved in their own congregations, who wanted to supplement their other religious activities with a small group that met regularly to talk about how a biblical faith could shape their practical lives. In a way, the recent Promise Keepers phenomenon has done a similar thing on a larger scale—calling men together from a variety of denominational traditions to form new patterns of fellowship and accountability.

But the parachurch pattern has also extended to a more task-oriented pattern. We evangelicals have founded a rich variety of evangelistic associations, summer Bible conferences, youth ministries, colleges and Bible institutes, mission agencies, Bible distribution societies, and the like—and we have seldom done so along strictly denominational lines. We have been concerned that the important tasks of the Christian community get done in the right manner, and the furthering of a specific denominational cause has seldom been a central motivation. Indeed, we have often reached out to other Christians by forming parachurch ministries precisely because we have not been happy with the ways in which established denominations perform—or fail to perform—what we see as important Christian tasks.

In our own way, then, we evangelicals have been very ecumenical in our eagerness to form liaisons across denominational lines. In this sense, we too have been a people who love the whole church, the entire household of the faithful. To be sure, we have been rather suspicious of the "organizational unity" endeavors of those Christians who are fond of inclusivist councils and denominational mergers. But that merely signals a commitment to a different style of ecumenism—one that emphasizes cooperation in common tasks, such as evangelism and mission.

Weaknesses and Strengths

Evangelicalism can be rightly criticized for many real shortcomings. We can't simply go back to the sawdust trail, not only because it belonged to another era, but because it really did foster some unhealthy traits and practices.

In my own efforts to work with others for the reform of the evangelical movement, I have concentrated on three common defects. The first is *anti-intellectualism.* Our deep commitment to experiential Christianity has often led us to express a rather strong distrust of the intellect. The second is *otherworldliness.* We have often been so pessimistic about the possibilities for healthy large-scale social change that we have been content to live on the margins of our culture, having become comfortable with a passive acceptance of the social, political, and economic status quo. And the third defect is *a separatistic spirit.* Our commitment to "getting the message out," combined with our emphasis on the local church, has led to considerable "false-witness bearing" toward other Christians. We have often not felt very accountable to Christian groups who are not immediately visible to us in our local worshiping community or who have not had obvious relevance to our evangelistic activities. And we have even been unspeakably harsh toward Christians with whom we have been closely linked, quibbling over doctrinal minutiae and exhibiting an ungracious and judgmental spirit about the behavior of others.

The awareness of these weaknesses has led some of us to devote considerable energy to the reform of the evangelical movement. And these efforts have been bearing fruit. In recent decades we have seen exciting new developments in evangelical scholarship, new programs of social activism, and a new evangelical openness to renewal movements taking place in other parts of the body of Christ.

Because weaknesses and strengths are often intimately connected, there is always a danger we will correct a weakness in such a way that we lose one of our strong points. I fear at times that we're vulnerable to this in evangelicalism. Take the three weaknesses I have just mentioned. Anti-intellectualism is a genuine danger, but so is a highly intellectualized packaging of Christianity. Otherworldliness is a threat to the Christian community, but so is a thoroughgoing this-worldliness. Ecclesiastical separatism is to be avoided, but we must also be on guard against a vague inclusivism in our understanding of Christian unity. We must monitor our own activity carefully, then, lest we embrace some defects that are as bad as—or even worse than—the ones we are trying to correct.

From time to time I hear the complaint that we evangelicals expend too much energy analyzing ourselves. We seem obsessed—or so the argument goes—with questions like, What *is* an evangelical? Where are we heading? How can we best preserve our evangelical identity?

I agree that too much introspection can be a bad thing. But I doubt that evangelicalism as a movement is in danger of falling into this trap. If anything, too few evangelicals these days are asking the self-critical questions—and as a result the questioners may begin to sound like they are overdoing it. But it is precisely because evangelicalism is a *movement* that self-examination is especially fitting. Movements need a sense of direction; they need to think about where they have been, where they are at present, and where they are going. There may come a time—even before the Lord returns!—when evangelicalism as a distinct branch of Christianity ought to go out of existence; we will only recognize that day when it comes, though, if we keep thinking about the *point* of the whole project.

And then, of course, there is the obvious fact that movements are groups of people who are in motion—which is why it is especially appropriate to call evangelicalism a movement. We are activists. Even when we were not very active in dealing with social issues, for example, it wasn't because we had chosen to be passive as such. We were busy with other things, such as evangelism, building churches, creating new ministries, and traveling far and wide as missionaries.

Holding Fast

I am not in favor of slowing us down. I know we need to keep moving. One of the valuable lessons I learned on the sawdust trail had to do with a sense of urgency. Religion isn't just an optional pastime. Doing the Lord's work is serious business. Issues of eternal significance are at stake. We may not have much time. Decide. Commit. Act.

All of this is important. But we must also *think* about what we are doing. We need a *mindful activism.* I like the way the writer to the Hebrews ties it together in his epistle: "Let us hold fast to our confession" (Hebrews 4:14 New Revised Standard Version). Elsewhere in the Bible we are told to "stand fast," but here the instruction is to *hold* fast. Holding fast is something you can do while you are moving fast. From the point of view of biblical Christianity, staying in motion is a thing to be valued. Saint Augustine rightly located it at the heart of our creaturely condition in the oft-quoted lines from the opening page of his *Confessions:* "Thou has made us for Thyself," he prayed, "and restless is our heart until it comes to rest in Thee." There is a sanctified restlessness that keeps us moving as we work toward the goals of God's kingdom. Sawdust trail people tend to move fast—new strategies to try, new fields to harvest, new regions to infiltrate with the gospel. But this kind of movement requires a clear sense of purpose. We need to be thinking clearly while we keep on the move.

As I continue on in my reflections on the heritage of the sawdust trail, it will be clear that these defects—anti-intellectualism, otherworldliness and the spirit of separatism—will be much on my mind, along with some others I will touch on along the way. The tendency toward displaying these defects can be seen quite clearly on the sawdust trail. But I also think that the sources for some good remedies can be found there. We can hold fast to the fundamental convictions of our past even as we "move fast" into the future.

CHAPTER FOUR

THE MAKING OF A CONVINCED EVANGELICAL

The Quakers have a nice way of dividing up their membership. They call the folks who grew up in the Society of Friends "birthright Quakers"; those who made a conscious choice to join they label "convinced Quakers." Well, I'm both a birthright evangelical and a convinced one. I was born into an evangelical family, but the "convincing" part came for me during the 1960s. For a few years in that decade I tried very hard not to be an evangelical. My strenuous efforts to shed my spiritual identity, however, were not successful. I finally came to the conclusion I was incurably evangelical.

Sawdust and Water

I was baptized as a baby at the First Holland Reformed Church of Passaic, New Jersey, my mother's home congregation. The members of that church were mainly first- and second-generation immigrants—in my childhood years a Dutch-language service was regularly held on Sunday afternoons.

Hardly a sawdust trail setting—or so it would seem. But the truth is that on the day of my baptism the smell of sawdust was in the air. My father, who didn't have a strong Christian upbringing, had experienced a dramatic conversion in his late teens at the Star of Hope Mission, a fundamentalist inner-city ministry in Paterson, New Jersey. Soon after accepting Jesus as his personal Savior he joined the staff of the Mission, preaching on street corners, in prisons, and in county medical care facilities. He was trained for this ministry in staff meetings where the Scofield Reference Bible was the primary textbook. When he met my mother, he was somewhat suspicious of her Dutch Reformed heritage.

On the Sunday of my baptism, my mother stood before the congregation, cradling me in her arms at the baptismal font; my father, who did not believe in infant baptism, sat in the front pew. He represented the sawdust trail at my baptism, looking on as a skeptical observer. My mother gratefully presented me to the church as "a covenant child." My father prayed I would someday realize that only a personal faith in Jesus, and not the rituals of the church, could guarantee my eternal salvation.

A few years later my father embarked on a formal program of theological education, and eventually he became a Reformed minister. But even though he changed his mind about infant baptism, there was always more than a hint of the smell of sawdust in his ministry. For example, the influence of the study notes in the Scofield Bible was always discernible in his preaching. And our family drew heavily on the spiritual resources of the fundamentalist world. We spent vacation time at Bible conferences listening to sermons on "Bible prophecy." We had family devotions where we read together from books published by Moody Press. We subscribed to fundamentalist magazines and listened to "gospel preaching" on the radio.

Many of my friends who study the history of sawdust trail happenings want to draw some clear boundaries among fundamentalism, the "holiness" movement, and Pentecostalism. We paid some attention to those distinctions when I was growing up—but we also crossed the lines on a regular basis. In all the places where my parents served pastorates they forged friendships with other local clergy couples. While these friends were almost never from the mainline churches, the scope was in its own way ecumenical: Wesleyan, Assemblies of God, Christian and Missionary Alliance, Conservative Baptist, Swedish Covenant. We attended their evangelistic crusades and revival services. I learned to sing Ira Sankey hymns sitting on folding chairs in "tent meetings" where there was still real sawdust on the ground. I have memories of lying on bunks in crude cabins at camp meetings where I could hear Wesleyans shouting praise to the Lord at "tarrying meetings" in the late hours of the night.

Fundamentalist Summers

During my high school years I worked for two summers on the kitchen crew at a fundamentalist Bible conference. At any given point some two hundred people—individuals, couples, families—stayed on the conference grounds, in a large hotel-type building, usually for a one-week or two-week stay. The staff was required to attend two services each day; the morning session was for Bible teaching, the evening for preaching. Each week brought a different roster of speakers; some of them were preachers from large fundamentalist churches, others were traveling evangelists, still others Bible institute faculty. The auditorium had dispensationalist charts on the walls. We sang a lot. Those of us who worked on the kitchen staff even sang hymns and gospel choruses together as we filled the dishwasher and scrubbed the pots and pans.

The teaching and preaching at the conference concentrated heavily on biblical content. But there were also regular condemnations of the ecumenical movement and of the "wolves in sheep's clothing" within the world of fundamentalist Christianity. One of the dangerous places mentioned regularly was a relatively new school in California—Fuller Theological Seminary.

Several years ago I attended a workshop in an eastern state. One Saturday there was nothing scheduled, so I took the hour-and-a-half drive to this Bible conference—my first visit back in over three decades. The place was still well kept, but it seemed almost deserted. As I walked into the registration area, a man who introduced himself as the director informed me that they had just completed a successful Youth Week, and they were preparing for an influx of conferees the next day. I gave my first name, and when I told him I had worked there as a teenager, he offered to walk the grounds with me.

As we strolled, I inquired about people from the conference's past. He was able to answer most of my questions. He also told me the sponsoring organization had recently added "fundamentalist" to its title "to show that we still stand for the truth in a time when there is so much liberalism, even in so-called 'evangelical' circles!" All of this was shared in friendly tones, and as we finished the tour I was hoping I could get away without altering the pleasant mood.

Before I got away, though, he initiated a line of questioning. I hoped—in vain—that each answer would be my last:

"Where are you from, Richard?"

"California."

"Oh—*where* in California?"

"The Los Angeles area."

"Are you a pastor?"

"No, I do some teaching."

"A Bible school?"

"Sort of—a seminary, actually."

"What do you teach?"

"Some philosophy courses. But, actually, I'm also the president."

"Oh—which seminary?"

"Fuller."

There was an awkward silence. Then in a noticeably less friendly voice he asked me my full name. I answered, and then I shook his hand again, thanked him for showing me around, and began to walk away. "Dr. Mouw," he called out. "Would you come in to sign our guest book? I'm sure our board members would be interested in knowing you were here."

I signed the book, and we shook hands again. "I owe this place a lot," I said. "Thanks again, and the Lord bless you." He did not return the blessing, but he thanked me for stopping by.

As I drove away, I felt very sad. I spent my time on the road thinking about the meaning of my sadness.

Affectionate Respect

A few weeks earlier, at the opening reception at an ecumenical gathering I was attending, I had been introduced to a woman who headed an agency at one of the more liberal Protestant denominations. She seemed genuinely friendly until she learned I was from Fuller Seminary, at which point she cooled markedly and quickly turned to talk with someone else.

I shed no tears on that occasion. That person probably had a somewhat distorted image of evangelicalism—at least of the sort I represent. But my guess is that even if she understood perfectly what I believe as an evangelical, she would still have strong disagreements with my views. When I run into negative responses from folks on the liberal side of the spectrum, my response is typically to shrug my shoulders and move on. If they want to have a friendly discussion, I'm game. If not, I won't expend much energy trying to engage them.

When fundamentalists treat me like a heretic, however, it gets to me in a deep place. Not that I'm always eager to engage fundamentalists in lengthy debates. As I walked the Bible conference grounds with my fundamentalist guide, I clearly wanted to avoid serious theological discussion at all cost. I knew I could not convince him of my wholehearted commitment to "biblical truth." There are too many things that go into his definitions of orthodoxy to which I simply could not subscribe. But it saddens me that this is the case—in a way that I am not troubled about my differences with a liberal Protestant.

Part of the reason, of course, is due to a family-type thing. I feel a debt of sorts to the fundamentalists. They helped to nurture me in the faith. It is a natural instinct to want some kind of approval from people who have mentored you along the way.

Yet, this really isn't the whole story. Calvin College provost Joel Carpenter puts it well in his recent historical study of twentieth-century fundamentalism. Carpenter, who is candid about his own affection for fundamentalism, looks at the movement from the perspective of an evangelical who wants to honor the movement's strengths while also exploring its weaknesses. "Fundamentalism was often intellectually lame, provincial, petty, mean-spirited, stultifying and manipulative," he observes, "but it could be enabling and energizing as well."[1]

I have spent a good part of my adult life concentrating on the glaring weaknesses of fundamentalism. In doing so, I haven't always been clear about the way in which it also has functioned as an "enabling and energizing" presence in my own life—and in the larger world of evangelical Christianity.

Books That Influence

No one has ever asked me to publish a list of the books that have most influenced me over the course of my life. I'm glad about that—not because I'm ashamed to identify the books, but because my list would look strange alongside the titles that scholars typically display. My guess is that when people compose those lists—

for a series that some magazine is running—it's natural to pick titles that require no elaboration. A professor of theology can list, say, Karl Barth's *Church Dogmatics* without needing to provide a rationale for the choice, but he might hesitate to put J. D. Salinger's *The Catcher in the Rye* on the same list without providing some autobiographical context for the choice.

In my case, the cynicism of Holden Caulfield, Salinger's teenage protagonist, was held in check by the examples of youthful rectitude provided for me in the fundamentalist novels I devoured in the years just before I came upon Salinger's book. The pious boys in those adventure stories had a faith in Christ that wasn't complicated by any hint of existential despair. But, then, Holden Caulfield showed no symptoms of a godly sorrow for sin. So when he tugged for my soul against the pull of the fictional teenage Christians, fortunately—even though Salinger's hero did put up a decent fight—the members of the Sugar Creek Gang won the spiritual tug-of-war.

In the course of my college studies I read many important books, and I'm sure that several of the classics—Plato's *The Republic*, Rousseau's *The Social Contract*, Thoreau's *Walden*—have had a significant impact on my intellectual development. But the books that really stand out in my mind were never assigned in any course; I simply happened to read them out of curiosity.

Here is a book that influenced me, even though I would not want to list it anywhere without at least a few words of explanation: Sinclair Lewis's *Elmer Gantry*, a novel about a fundamentalist evangelist whose private life did not—to put it mildly—fit very nicely with his public preaching. During my freshman year of college, I had hitchhiked to a nearby city to attend a "healing crusade" conducted by Pentecostal evangelist A. A. Allen. I came away questioning the integrity of what I had seen and heard. Allen seemed to me to be drunk (a suspicion that, given some later reports about his life and ministry, turned out not to be farfetched), and I had grave doubts about at least one of the "miracles" I had observed that evening: a blind man, with two artificial glass eyeballs who claimed, after Allen laid hands on his head, that he could now see clearly.

It was soon after this experience that I read—indeed, on the recommendation of a friend to whom I had reported my A. A. Allen experience—Sinclair Lewis's novel. It did not make me completely distrusting of evangelists; I've never had a moment's doubt, for example, about Billy Graham's integrity (or about the power of his message). But the novel did put me in a frame of mind to distance myself from the more emotional aspects of fundamentalist piety.

There were more serious books, however. Two of them have to be paired together, since they functioned as an important point-counterpoint on a basic theological matter. The first was Harry Emerson Fosdick's *A Guide to Understanding the Bible*, a book I read as a mild act of rebellion. I had heard Fosdick's name mentioned many times by preachers and Bible teachers, and it was always used as a symbol of all that was evil about modernist theology. So when I saw his book in a bookstore and immediately purchased it, I felt like I was partaking of forbidden fruit. I found his ideas to be fascinating reading. He depicted the religion of the Old Testament in evolutionary terms: Early on the Jews saw Yahweh (a name that was new to me; in my heart I still think of Jehovah as God's "real" name) as a local deity—one among many—who operated with a primitive need to be placated by blood sacrifices; gradually this sense of the divine was revised and expanded, as Fosdick told the story, until it reached its fruition in the life of Jesus, who both taught and modeled a universal love.

I was not completely convinced by his thesis, but reading his book proved to be a stimulating intellectual adventure. And I began to make use of some of Fosdick's themes in discussions with my fundamentalist friends at the Christian liberal arts college I was attending. During a visit home, I had a long conversation with a newly ordained Reformed pastor who was fond of the writings being produced by faculty members of Westminster Theological Seminary. When I tried my Fosdick-type explorations out on him, he merely smiled, reaching for a book on a shelf in his study. "Here, take this and read it—it is much more rigorous than Fosdick."

The book was Edward J. Young's *Thy Word Is Truth*. Young made a strong case for biblical inerrancy—but in a manner much different from the kind of fundamentalist rhetoric to which I was accustomed. He took seriously the claims the biblical writers make about their own authority, and he insisted—and this is the point I found most compelling—that how you read the Bible depends a great deal on the presuppositions you bring to the text. A few years later I read James I. Packer's *"Fundamentalism" and the Word of God*, where Packer took a similar conception of revelation and compared it at length with the perspectives of Catholicism and Protestant liberalism. The basic understanding of a "high" view of the Bible's authority, as set forth in these books by Young and Packer, took hold in my mind and heart—and it continues (with some modifications made over the years) to be the way I view such matters.

Cultic Orthodoxy

Another important book for me was Edward John Carnell's *The Case for Orthodox Theology*. In the late 1950s a mainline Protestant publisher announced that it was publishing three different orthodox "cases," authored by prominent theologians—a liberal Protestant, a neo-orthodox thinker, and an evangelical. The identities of the writers were kept secret for a time, so there was some curiosity in the evangelical world about who would be representing our perspective. When Carnell's book appeared I bought it immediately. Even as I was reading it, the president of our college gave a special chapel talk in which he strongly criticized Carnell for betraying the evangelical cause.

The section of the book that caused the most controversy was actually my favorite. In a chapter titled "Perils," Carnell singled out fundamentalism—which he characterized as "orthodoxy gone cultic"—for lengthy criticism. And he did so with a tone that brought delight to the hearts of evangelical college students who were chafing under the restrictions against various forms of "worldliness." We enjoyed reading some of Carnell's passages out loud to our friends. Here are a few of our favorites:

> When the fundamentalist develops his ethical code, he is somewhat prompted by status in the cult. Consequently, he defines the good life as the separated life—separated, that is, from prevailing social mores. Whereas Christ was virtuous because he loved God with all his heart and his neighbor as himself, the fundamentalist is virtuous because he does not smoke, dance, or play cards. By raising a scrupulous demur over social mores, the fundamentalist can divert attention from grosser sins—anger, jealousy, hatred, gossip, lust, idleness, malice, backbiting, schism, guile, injustice, and every shade of illicit pride.

> The fundamentalist is ... very certain that movie attendance is sinful, for the movie industry is a tool of Satan. But when the fundamentalist judges films on television, he uses a radically different standard. There is a cultic reason for this shift in standards. Fundamentalists, it so happens, are afraid of one another. If a fundamentalist is seen entering a theater, he may be tattled on by a fellow fundamentalist. In this event the guilty party would "lose his testimony," i.e., his status in the cult would be threatened. But when he watches movies on television, this threat does not exist. Drawn shades keep prying eyes out. One of the unexpected blessings of television is that it lets the fundamentalist catch up on all the movies he missed on religious principles.[2]

The fact that Edward Carnell was associated with Fuller Seminary, even serving for a time as its president, signaled to many of us that there was a way out of fundamentalism without our needing to become liberals. If fundamentalism was "orthodoxy gone cultic," then what we needed to do was to preserve the "orthodoxy" while at the same time purging it of the "cultic" accretions. This is what Carnell—and the larger "neo-evangelicalism" represented by Fuller, Christianity Today, and a number of other organizations that were distancing themselves from the older fundamentalism—promised to make possible. I found the promise an exciting one. I wanted to work hard at helping to fulfill it. I still see this project as an extremely worthy one.

Leaving and Returning

Earlier I mentioned that during my graduate school days I did spend a few years trying not to be an evangelical. My struggles had to do with the *applicability* of evangelical theology to a strange new world I encountered as I moved from an evangelical college campus to the secular university campus.

Watching the televised coverage of Martin Luther King's "I Have a Dream" speech—delivered just days before I started my graduate studies—had a profound impact on me. What Dr. King was calling for, a justice that would roll down like a mighty river, struck me as so clearly biblical that I could not imagine any Christian denying the legitimacy and power of his witness. Yet the evangelicals I knew—including many leaders I had come to respect on other grounds—were often dismissive of, and in some cases even hostile to, the civil rights movement.

My disillusionment increased as I began to wrestle in my conscience with questions about the war in Southeast Asia. Here too the evangelical community seemed incapable of comprehending why so many of us struggled with the issue of military involvement. On some basic questions of right and wrong, I found secular sources to be more helpful than evangelical ones. So I drifted away. I saw myself as a spiritual exile.

I explored alternative worldviews. While I was joining political protests, I also was enrolled in advanced courses in social thought and ethics. I attended churches—ecumenical chapel services, Catholic masses, liberal Protestant congregations—where the "big" moral issues were dealt with at length and in depth. I read extensively in "social gospel" and "radical discipleship" literature. I learned much in and through all of this—but I found little to satisfy me in the deep places of my soul. I had some new moral convictions, but I wanted to *ground* them in a larger understanding of the way things are.

A case in point: The major theme song of the civil rights movement was "We Shall Overcome." When I saw people joining hands to sing this song, often in situations where the threat of violence against them was very real, I was inspired. But I also wanted to know more about the *basis* of the hope that was expressed so passionately in the song. *Why* the strong conviction that this particular cause is the winning one? Many of these folks were secularists. Where would they derive the strength to carry the battle forward even after serious setbacks? What made them so sure that nonviolent protest was the best way to bring about moral change?

My questions were not silly ones. Many of these folks did finally give up on their commitments to nonviolence. Some of them became cynical about any attempts to change "the system." Others went on to follow more destructive courses of action.

I knew what grounding I needed in order to be sustained in my moral commitments. "We *shall* overcome"—but only because Jesus Christ has overcome sin and death. And I was not satisfied with vague formulations about what this meant. For me moral hope was possible only because of a "bodily resurrection"—a real body came out of a real tomb on Easter morning.

Not only did I want to make connections between social action and Christian "fundamentals," but I also discovered that whenever I got into a mood of basic questioning of the social-political-economic status quo, I drew my basic inspiration from the piety of evangelicalism. The rhetoric of fundamentalist "altar calls" and "invitation hymns" called for a comprehensive kind of self-examination, lest we hold back some area of our lives from complete submission to Jesus: "Is your all on the altar of sacrifice laid?" "Lord of all or not Lord at all!" "I surrender all." But the "all-ness" that evangelicals had proclaimed typically applied to a somewhat restricted area of sinfulness. We had to be sure our sex lives and personal habits and financial dealings were placed under the Lord's control. But I now started to pose the evangelical questions about more "corporate" concerns. Why shouldn't our draft cards be placed on the altar of sacrifice? Shouldn't Jesus be made the Lord of what we do when we enter the voting booth? Mustn't we surrender our racism, our fondness for military solutions, and our ethnocentrism to his control?

All of these thoughts were solidified for me one afternoon as I fiddled with the radio dial in our student apartment in Chicago. Searching for a newscast, I came upon WMBI, the Moody Bible Institute station. The Moody Chorale was singing hymns, and I decided to listen for a while. The hymn that got through to me was an oldie I hadn't heard for several years:

> There is a fountain filled with blood
> Drawn from Immanuel's veins;
> And sinners, plunged beneath that flood,
> Lose all their guilty stains.

I've told the story many times about how the hearing of this hymn affected me—but I've always told it with a little bit of awkwardness. On several occasions I have not gotten past quoting the first line before I have seen some folks—even some evangelical folks—roll their eyes, clearly signaling their distaste for the imagery. So I have often made a point of covering myself at the outset by saying something like this: "I wish the Holy Spirit had used a different hymn, but who am I to question the Spirit's ways!" The truth is, though, that my defensive comment is not a very honest one. I actually like the hymn. That day, listening to the Moody Chorale, I found it deeply moving, and I still do.

I am emboldened to admit this because of the delightful little meditation on this hymn I recently read. In his book *Brightest and Best: Stories of Hymns*, Father George Rutler tells about listening to this hymn during his boyhood. Rutler, who made the move not too long ago from the Anglican to the Roman Catholic priesthood, reports that when he was growing up in New Jersey he would look forward to the annual midsummer tent meetings sponsored by the local evangelicals. He would watch them pitch the large tent—and spread real sawdust on the ground. While Rutler's Episcopalian inhibitions kept him from actually going into the tent, he did stand outside to listen to the lively singing. "There Is a Fountain" is one hymn he especially "enjoyed for its excellence and its power to shock squeamish piety." In its boldness the hymn echoes, says Rutler, a more ancient anthem:

> "In that day there shall be a fountain opened to the house of David and to the inhabitants of Jerusalem for sin and for uncleanness" (Zechariah 13:1). [William] Cowper had the sense to celebrate the fulfillment of this prophecy on Calvary by giving us a hymn about blood that stirs the blood.[3]

My blood was indeed stirred as I heard the Moody Chorale sing about the blood that was shed on Calvary. I felt like I was discovering for the first time the real power of an evangelical faith. Nothing I had been studying in recent years, both in my philosophy courses and in my personal search for a way of tying things together—no secular perspective, no social gospel theology, no tract on "political Christianity"—had the radical depth of the solution the Moody choir was singing about. *All* of our guilty stains! Not only the very real guilty stains of my personal life but also the stains of our racism and nationalism and militarism. I knew, in that very moment, that while I had to keep wrestling with many of the trappings of evangelicalism, I had no choice but to do so *as* an evangelical.

CHAPTER FIVE

MINDFUL EVANGELICALISM

On a wintry day in 1970 I drove from my Michigan home to the University of Chicago campus. Late in the afternoon my doctoral committee would give me my final "oral exam" for the Ph.D. degree in Philosophy. It was one of the most important days of my academic career, and I did not want to be late for the meeting, so I arrived with several hours to spare. As I wandered around the campus where I had studied full-time for three years, I was very apprehensive. While it's a normal thing to be nervous on a day like this, I knew I had no good reason to worry about passing this final test. I had done consistently well in my program and had received strong signals that my committee members were positive about my dissertation. The worst that could happen, I assured myself, was that I might let my nervousness show too much or that the committee would require me to make a few minor revisions in one of my chapters.

But I was still apprehensive. With plenty of time on my hands, I found a coffee shop and sat there collecting my thoughts. As I reflected on my mood, I came to a rather surprising conclusion: *I was feeling guilty.* Some voice deep inside was telling me that in going through with this final stage of the process, I was cheating the university. I wasn't the kind of person who should be earning a Ph.D. in philosophy. If my secular professors knew what my real convictions were about the basic issues of life, they would simply fail me, no matter how profound a dissertation I might have written.

I also detected another voice accusing me of wrongdoing. This one was a very Christian voice, one whose tones also evoked memories of the smell of sawdust. It spoke the familiar language of a long line of preachers, Bible teachers, and evangelists. "You have compromised with the world," this voice said. "You have followed ways of thinking that are not fitting for a child of God. When you successfully clear this final hurdle, it is Satan who will claim the real victory."

Two very different voices—one speaking from the secular academy, the other from the sawdust trail. But their message to me was the same: *Shame on you for what you are about to achieve!*

Of course, I knew better than to accept these accusing voices at face value. I was already teaching at Calvin College, a school with a strong reputation for both careful scholarship and impeccable biblical orthodoxy. When a few years earlier I had reported to one of my University of Chicago professors—a secular Jew—that I had accepted an appointment to the philosophy faculty at Calvin College, he beamed and told me I was joining "the best undergraduate philosophy department in the country." The Calvin campus was a place where piety and learning were joined in a marvelous way. On one level, I was very secure in my identity as a Christian scholar—which is why I was so surprised that the accusing voices spoke so loudly to me that day on the Chicago campus. I thought I had long ago silenced them.

Asking Questions

When I was a student at a large public high school in New Jersey I belonged to a teenage Bible club, comprised of students from our school who got together regularly to encourage each other in our Christian walk. One day an alumna of our little group came back to visit us. She had graduated from our high school the year before and was now a student at a large public university. She was home on her spring break, and she visited our group to tell us what it was like to be a Christian on a secular university campus.

I will never forget her testimony. She told us about a philosophy course she was taking. It was a very weird subject, she said. The professor tried to get them to ask questions like, What is truth? What is goodness? What is reality? At one point in the course, she reported, he had even asked them to think about whether the desks in the room continued to exist when no one was perceiving them.

We agreed with her—this was indeed pretty weird stuff. We shook our heads in disbelief that anyone could waste their time with such strange thoughts. And then she said something that made a deep impression on me. "I'm glad I'm a Christian," she said, "because that means I don't have to worry about such things. When you know that Christ is the answer, then you don't have to worry about the questions!"

I remember my reaction well. I was inspired by her straightforward and unadorned faith. And I silently prayed I too would always have the kind of simple confidence that would keep me from being carried away by philosophical speculation.

But alas, it was not to be. When I became a college student I voraciously consumed all of the philosophy courses that were available. Those questions she thought were so strange suddenly came alive for me. I even got to the point where I found it quite interesting to argue about whether the desk in my room continued to exist when no one was perceiving it!

I must confess, though, that for a long time I felt guilty about the philosophical bent I had developed. I measured myself against this young woman's simple faith, and I found myself wanting. But, thank God, I finally made my peace as a Christian with the idea of a questioning spirit. I came to see that Jesus is not only the Answer, but that he is also the great Questioner. And I learned that it is important for the health of the evangelical movement that we—some of us, at least—be encouraged to ask fundamental and difficult questions.

I once heard British evangelist John Stott give a nice description of the need for a disciplined and questioning Christian intellect. Bible-believing Christians, Stott said, must be "conservative radicals." We must be *conservative* in the sense that we are absolutely committed to conserving the truth of God's Word. And we must be *radical* in the sense that, from the perspective of being firmly grounded in the eternal message of the infallible Word of God that points us to Jesus Christ as our supreme authority—from that foundational perspective—we must be willing to subject everything else to critical scrutiny. Needless to say, Stott isn't calling for a spirit of uninterrupted negativism—which is important to emphasize in our day, when deconstructionists and other devotees of "postmodernity" often celebrate a thoroughgoing negativism. Subjecting things to critical scrutiny—a standing back from that which most people take for granted—is an important exercise to engage in on occasion, but it is not meant to be a way of life. The goal of a healthy questioning spirit is to achieve a clarity about the things that matter most; it is not to cultivate an attitude of sheer negativity.

At a Fuller faculty meeting a few years ago, a colleague made an important speech in which he called all of us to be more prayerful. "If everyone at Fuller Seminary would pray even three minutes a day," he said, " think of how much spiritual power would be injected into our community!" I fully supported his plea, but it also gave me an idea for a parallel request. I waited a month or so, so as not to detract from his passionate expression of spiritual concern, and then I made a public plea of my own: "If everyone at Fuller Seminary would think clearly about something—about anything that happens to come to mind—for only three minutes a day," I said, "think of how much intellectual power would be injected into the universe from this campus!"

It was this conviction that clear thinking is important to the health of the Christian community that had led me to pursue graduate study in philosophy. By the time I drove to Chicago for my final oral examination, I had come to see this as the natural way for Christians to view things. And that's why I was so surprised about the struggle in my soul as I walked the University of Chicago campus that wintry day in 1970.

Anti-intellectual Themes

The college student who talked to our high school Bible club was saying the kind of thing one could hear on a regular basis on the sawdust trail. The evangelists and revival preachers of my youth proclaimed their anti-intellectualism with great passion. Some of their slogans have stuck with me: "Don't even bother getting an education unless you know how to get the victory over it!" "The only school any Christian ever has to enroll in is the Holy Ghost School of the Bible!" "You don't need a lot of exegesis. All you need is Jesus!"

These folks were poking fun at intellectuals, and it's easy to poke some fun back at what they said and believed. But to do so can divert us from a necessary understanding of the deeper impulses at work in this anti-intellectual rhetoric. In order to see what's going on beneath the surface, we need to adopt a charitable attitude and explore the history of this way of viewing things.

The history of pietism is the place to start. The pietists were engaged in an ongoing struggle against intellectualism. The first stage of this struggle we alluded to earlier. The pietist movement began as a reaction against the "head knowledge" of preachers who were quite orthodox but who had so intellectualized the faith that their sermons seemed to be nothing more than lengthy theological lectures. The pietists' souls were not being fed by two-hour discourses in which various doctrinal formulations about the Trinity were shown to be defective, or where the idea of an "equal ultimacy of election and reprobation" was defended in great detail. So they formed their house churches where matters of "the heart" were emphasized and the practical challenges of discipleship were discussed in terms that even uneducated folks could get excited about.

But then there was a second stage in the pietists' struggle against intellectualism. This time the enemy was not "dead orthodoxy" but a heterodoxy—a set of non-Christian teachings—that was very much alive in the surrounding culture. The universities became the strongholds of "Enlightenment" thinking, which celebrated the power of unaided human reason to solve all of the problems of human existence. This way of viewing things made inroads into the churches. *Reason* became the reference point for deciding all issues of truth and goodness and meaning. In the nineteenth century this theological perspective came to be known as *Modernism*. People who were truly "modern," who were in touch with the flow of history, could no longer accept the outmoded ideas associated with a belief in a universe actively ruled by a personal God.

I once came across a published sermon from the beginning of this century, written by a preacher who was obviously caught up in this Modernist spirit. His text was the story of the loaves and the fish, and at the beginning of the sermon he assured his congregation that no intelligent person these days could possibly believe that Jesus somehow increased the supply of food by some "magical" act. Here's what really happened, said the preacher: Everyone in the crowd that day had actually brought their lunches with them, but they kept them hidden under their robes because they selfishly refused to consider sharing with others. Except for this one boy! In his childlike innocence he brought his lunch to Jesus, hoping against hope that the Master would be able to use it to feed the crowd. And he was right. Jesus used the example of the boy's selflessness to shame the selfish adults. They then all pulled out their lunches and began to share with others, and, lo and behold, there was more than enough to go around. Thus the real "miracle" here was the boy's simple trust in the power of sharing with others.

From an evangelical perspective this interpretation would be sheer silliness if it weren't also such dangerous theology. If you think the belief that Jesus could multiply loaves and fish is a piece of superstition, then you have problems with some fundamental biblical teachings. God created the world out of the formless void. He created life in a virgin's womb. He brought Jesus back from the dead. In short, the God of the Bible is in the business of producing good things out of nothing. Once you believe that truth, multiplying loaves and fish is one of God's easier performances—he didn't even have to start from scratch in this case!

The pietists and their fellow travelers were right to worry about what intellectual types were capable of doing once they decided to apply their rational schemes to religion. Dead orthodoxy and living heterodoxy are indeed serious threats to a vibrant Christian faith.

Some Good Instincts

Let me be clear about my bias: I get paid to defend Christian higher education. But I also don't accept pay to defend things I don't agree with. I believe in Christian colleges and seminaries. I want Christians to learn to think clearly. I want pastors and missionaries and therapists and lawyers to understand the details of a Christian worldview.

As a seminary president I spend a lot of time explaining to people why they ought to support theological education. This kind of apologetic comes easy for me. I am convinced a healthy church needs leaders who can read the Bible in the original languages, who can explain difficult passages in the Book of Revelation, who understand the heresies that threatened the church in the fourth century after Christ, who write books about the life of John Wesley, who can explain why Jehovah's Witnesses are wrong when they attack the doctrine of the Trinity ... and on and on.

But for all of that, I try to understand the anti-intellectual impulses in evangelicalism, and I work hard at not being shocked at or offended by them. I pay special attention to what is going on when people express skepticism about the need for seminaries. The historic reasons for the pietist distrust of the academy, as I have already described them, are obvious factors. But there are other instincts at work. One such instinct is connected to a deep commitment to effective ministry. We evangelicals know that theological education has all too often had the effect of dampening spiritual ardor. Theological schools have sometimes fostered a clerical elitism that is out of touch with the spiritual needs of ordinary Christians. I know that when evangelicals have questioned the need for formal theological education, it has typically been out of a devotion to a high, rather than a low, view of the ministerial calling.

And I have to face the fact that some Christians have engaged in wonderful ministries without any kind of formal training. One of my heroines in the faith, for example, is Corrie ten Boom (I'll discuss her again later). She learned profound lessons about what it means to trust and obey the Lord from her very practical experiences in protecting Jews from the Nazis and then being sent to a concentration camp. Out of those experiences she shaped a ministry of serving Jesus that has touched thousands of lives. That she never earned a degree in theology matters nothing to me. I admire her greatly and have learned much from her writings.

A closely related instinct has to do with a sense of *urgency* about doing the Lord's work. The pressure of the urgent has often been associated, for example, with the missionary movement: "O Zion, haste, thy mission high fulfilling." This should not surprise us, since the missionary movement has been caught up in matters that are indeed urgent. The Christian community has received a direct mandate from the Lord to carry the gospel to the nations (see Matthew 28:19–20). Eternal destinies are at stake. To such a mandate haste is a highly appropriate response.

Again, both of these instincts are good ones. Not everyone who wants to serve the Lord effectively needs to have formal education. Indeed, there are some gifted people in the Christian community whom *we* should study rather than insist that they engage in studies. But to make this assertion points to the need for at least some of us to be engaged in research and teaching. The lessons we can learn from gifted leaders need to be written down and passed on to others. Not everyone can draw on the kind of natural talent and resources that were available to a Corrie ten Boom or a Mother Teresa. They are like musical prodigies who somehow know how to play the piano brilliantly with little formal training. It's not the normal way in which great pianists reach their peak. The rest of us need to read the guidebooks and manuals that can be produced by observing the "natural" geniuses at work.

Nor is there a contradiction involved in both acknowledging the urgent challenges of ministry and also engaging in unhurried, reflective *discussion* about these matters of extreme urgency.

Hospital emergency rooms are places where urgent activity is always occurring. Haste is usually a necessity when dealing with medical crises. But emergency rooms need to be supported by careful, unhurried academic research. The medical experts who go into action when the ambulance arrives can do their work well only because medical researchers work patiently in laboratories and attend scholarly conferences, and because doctors and nurses spend more than a few years sitting in classrooms. And the same can be said for the urgent tasks of preaching, counseling, evangelizing, and feeding the hungry. We need to back up the spiritual ambulance drivers and emergency room nurses with careful, biblically faithful theological reflection.

Some Advances

It is over a half century since theologian Carl Henry published his important little book titled *The Uneasy Conscience of Modern Fundamentalism*. In this brief manifesto Henry offered a trenchant critique of the "world flight" patterns displayed in the older fundamentalism's indifference to social ills. But Henry gave no comfort to those people in his day who wanted conservative Protestantism to correct its ethical maladies simply by launching programs of social reform. He discerned that the evangelical lack of a sense of social responsibility was rooted in an inadequate perspective on culture and in a closely related failure to develop strong intellectual habits. His corrective prescriptions, then, were heavily weighted in favor of educational and scholarly strategies. He urged evangelicals to "develop a competent literature in every field of study, on every level from the grade school through the university, which adequately presents each subject with its implications from the Christian as well as non-Christian points of view.... Evangelicalism must contend for a fair hearing for the Christian mind, among other minds, in secular education."[1]

It should be obvious that we still have a long way to go before we fully achieve the rather ambitious intellectual goals Carl Henry set for evangelicals in 1947. But it should also be obvious that we have come a long way from the intellectually and culturally impoverished state of affairs in the evangelicalism out of which he wrote some fifty-plus years ago. For one thing, evangelicals have produced an impressive array of scholarly organizations devoted to intradisciplinary dialogue: the Society of Christian Philosophers, the Faith and History group, the American Scientific Affiliate, the Christianity and Literature organization, and similar groups composed of political scientists, sociologists, economists, and so on—to say nothing of the interdisciplinary projects and scholarly efforts made possible by new patterns of cooperation in the network of evangelical colleges and seminaries.

A few years ago two books were published, each by a respected evangelical scholar, which discussed at length the present state of evangelical intellectual life. Each book received quite a bit of attention. Wheaton College professor Mark Noll began *The Scandal of the Evangelical Mind* by describing the book as "an epistle from a wounded lover" who has frequently suspected that "it is simply impossible to be, with integrity, both evangelical and intellectual."[2] He went on to provide a detailed account of the obstacles to the intellectual life evangelicals have erected.

British theologian Alister McGrath looked at the issue from a somewhat different angle in his *Evangelicalism and the Future of Christianity*. While he made it clear that he is not insensitive to the dangers of evangelical anti-intellectualism, he also expressed real worries about the threat of a new rationalism that could easily invade the evangelical camp, as it did in the post-Reformation generation. To stave off the danger that comes with evangelicalism's "increasing intellectual sophistication," Dr. McGrath is convinced we must continue to emphasize the experiential dimensions of the Christian life, as well as to respond to the need to call contemporary men and women into a vital relationship with the heaven-sent Savior. Again, none of this is to deny the need for careful scholarship and clear thinking. But we can best meet this need by keeping alive a vision of Christian wholeness "in which theologians are evangelists and evangelists theologians."[3]

Both books make an important point. Mark Noll rightly complains about the continuing signs of anti-intellectualism in the evangelical community, while Alister McGrath rightly points to the dangers of moving too far in the other direction. I take both warnings seriously. I hope we never stop attending to both concerns, even though to do so will require that we live with some discomforting tensions. In my own personal journey, to live with this tension means I must continually remind myself not to complain when the voices from the sawdust trail accuse me in those moments when I think I deserve to be enjoying my intellectual accomplishments.

FUNDAMENTALISM
REVISITED

During the past decade or so I have occasionally played around with a rather perverse theological fantasy. I have thought of announcing the formation of yet another "neo" movement within evangelicalism—this one I would label "neo-fundamentalism." I hasten to repeat: It is a mere fantasy, and admittedly a perverse one. But there is nonetheless a germ of seriousness for me in the idea.

The thoughts that sparked the fantasy came shortly after current Notre Dame professor George Marsden published his much-acclaimed history of Fuller Seminary titled *Reforming Fundamentalism.* A person who was quite fond of Fuller told me he liked the Marsden book very much but found the title "embarrassing." This wasn't a word I would have thought to use, so I pressed him for clarification. He explained that he had rejected his fundamentalist upbringing and now looked to Fuller for "a more sophisticated evangelicalism." But to make a big thing about Fuller's connection to a fundamentalist past, he said—well, it was for him "embarrassing." Much better, as he viewed things, to reject fundamentalism altogether than to be associated with any effort to "reform" it.

Prior to this conversation, I hadn't thought much about the Marsden title. But now I began to muse about what it means to "reform" something. It would be very strange, for example, to give the title "Reforming Roman Catholicism" to a book about the Protestant Reformation. When the sixteenth-century Reformers set out to change things, they broke completely with the Roman church. They were re-forming (re-making, re-establishing) the church as such—a church that, as they saw things, had gotten completely messed up in Catholic hands. When a group within a particular political party, on the other hand, announces that it is working for the reform of their party, they are not trying to create a brand-new entity but rather to renew the existing party from within. They are working on something they see as seriously damaged—but they are also convinced it is worth fixing.

The person who expressed annoyance with Professor Marsden's book title would have been happy, I'm sure, with "Reforming Evangelicalism" as an alternative. This person saw fundamentalism as a distorted version of the evangelical movement. To attempt a repair job on fundamentalism was, for him, a waste of time. He saw Fuller Seminary as embodying a new kind of evangelicalism—one purged of fundamentalist distortions.

My own criticisms of fundamentalism are probably quite similar to his. But I do have a difficult time seeing the fundamentalists as nothing more than the villains in the story of evangelical reform.

Survival and Beyond

I must confess that in my own support for the "neo-evangelical" cause I have often engaged in a bit of fundamentalist-bashing. This is why it was good for my soul to read Joel Carpenter's *Revive Us Again: The Reawakening of American*

Fundamentalism, a compelling account and an honest assessment of what happened to American fundamentalism from 1930 to 1950. Professor Carpenter's book picks up the story where George Marsden left off in his much-discussed 1980 book titled *Fundamentalism and American Culture: The Shaping of Twentieth-Century Evangelicalism, 1870-1925*. Together these two books provide an excellent and authoritative history of the fundamentalist movement.

As the conventional wisdom had it at the time, Protestant fundamentalism was all but dead by the end of the 1920s. The fundamentalists had struggled for several decades against "modernizing" tendencies in old-line Protestantism, and now they had, to all appearances, lost the battle. Their efforts to gain control of denominational seminaries and missionary agencies had failed, and one of their most visible champions, William Jennings Bryan, had suffered a humiliating defeat in the infamous J. T. Scopes "monkey trial" in 1925.

Twenty-five years later, however, the fundamentalist cause was very much alive and well. What happened between 1930 and 1950 to bring about a reversal in fundamentalism's fortunes? This is the story Joel Carpenter tells so well. Like Professor Marsden, he sees fundamentalism as a movement full of "paradoxical tensions." Not the least of these has to do with the fundamentalists' basic understanding of their place in North American culture. The Puritan notion of America as having a special divine appointment among the nations is deeply embedded in the fundamentalists' collective psyche. But the nineteenth-century Darwinian crisis and (not unrelated) the increasing influence of secularism in American public life brought about a strong sense of cultural transition that, as Marsden argued, was not unlike an immigrant experience. In this case the migration was not one of literal geography, but as evangelical Protestants moved into the twentieth century they felt like they were somehow being transported into a strange new land. They were moving from the New Israel to the New Babylon.

The battles against theological modernism during the first thirty years of the twentieth century only served to reinforce this mood of cultural pessimism. Having lost the struggle for control of the old-line denominations, the fundamentalists came to see their role in the larger culture in "remnant" terms: They were the faithful cognitive minority who possessed inside "prophetic" information about the world's inevitable decline toward doom. The only hope for the future was the ushering in of a supernaturally initiated millennial kingdom. In the meantime, the faithful remnant must concentrate on the work of spiritual rescue by means of evangelizing the lost and providing spiritual nurture for the remnant. And that is precisely what the fundamentalists worked at for two decades. And in doing so—as it turns out—they guaranteed their survival. Indeed, they did more than survive. They prepared the way for a vital evangelicalism that would come to function in recent decades as an influential movement in the Christian world in particular and in the larger American cultural scene in general.

Correcting an Overreaction

What does all of this have to do with my perverse theological fantasy about a "neo-fundamentalist" movement? At the heart of this fantasy is the growing recognition that in all of my efforts to prove I have long ago abandoned fundamentalist traits and convictions, I have failed to acknowledge my indebtedness to— and my continuities with—the fundamentalism that nurtured me in my early years.

Joel Carpenter hits home with the criticisms he makes of folks like me. Take the case of Edward John Carnell. Earlier I mentioned my glee, as a college student, over the way Dr. Carnell attacked the fundamentalists in his *The Case for Orthodox Theology*. Characterizing fundamentalism as "orthodoxy gone cultic," he chided the movement for the pettiness of many of its attitudes and legalisms.

There is a certain measure of naivete embodied in these criticisms of fundamentalism, argues Professor Carpenter. All religious movements that are trying to accomplish something important are necessarily "cultic." A movement needs to forge an identity, which means establishing behavioral and cognitive boundaries. This is turn means devising, as Carpenter puts it, "'mores and symbols' to live by, and these, by their very nature as human fabrications, reflect the circumstances of their makers."[1] Furthermore, says Carpenter, Carnell and his colleagues failed to acknowledge that in their efforts to improve on what the fundamentalists had done, they were making use of the very subculture they were attempting to alter. While the fundamentalists could certainly be "intellectually lame, provincial, petty, mean-spirited, stultifying and manipulative,"[2] they also managed to produce a new generation—people like Carnell—who were not at all attracted to liberalism but who were restless to bring new intellectual and evangelistic energy to the larger vision they had received from their fundamentalist forebears.

Carpenter rightly reminds us that those "who chide a prior generation for not seeing its own foibles and limitations should know that some day their descendents will say the same of them."[3] But he is not content simply to have us tolerate the fundamentalists' shortcomings; he wants us to see their very real strengths: "They were able to create close-knit and supportive fellowships. They had plenty of outlets for inventiveness and entrepreneurial expansion, and they enjoyed life-changing religious experiences that came to them in forms and language they had fashioned."[4] In a day when "fundamentalist" has become a label that gets thrown around with much abandon by the folks who take delight in disparaging strong religious convictions, many of us can be grateful that the fundamentalists taught us some important lessons about what it means to be caught up in passionate witness.

Organizational Savvy

Joel Carpenter also points us to the organizational savvy of fundamentalism. Much of his narrative focuses on the intricate subculture the fundamentalists constructed to implement their mission. While the secularizing elites took it for granted that "the old-time religion" was a thing of the past, the fundamentalists were building a complex system of independent organizations—youth ministries, evangelistic teams, Bible institutes, seminaries, missionary agencies, summer Bible conferences, Bible distribution societies, and so on. These organizations were somewhat eclectic theologically; advocates of the "Old Princeton" brand of Presbyterian Calvinism managed to cooperate in various settings with both the more "Bible prophecy" oriented dispensational theologians and the relatively atheological "get the message out" pragmatists. The fundamentalist subculture was surprisingly transdenominational, with participants representing the newer independent "Bible churches" as well as pockets of conservatism within the more established denominational bodies.

During the period when the fundamentalists were building this organizational infrastructure, the old-line Protestant bodies seemed content to maintain the more traditional denominational patterns. Their efforts at creating new interdenominational networks focused primarily on leadership-oriented "council of churches" entities, in contrast to the fundamentalists' less "official" grassroots networks.

In all of this, the liberals were oblivious to the fact that they were being outflanked by the theological opponents they thought they had defeated in earlier battles. Although the process was not very visible for several decades, the fundamentalists were, as Joel Carpenter puts it, helping to affect "a major shift among the basic institutional carriers of American religious life."[5] The results are quite obvious today. Many commentators even insist we are in a "postdenominational" era. While this may be overstated, there can be no doubt that, as Carpenter observes, the old-line "denominations have been losing members, income, and influence while special-purpose, non-denominational religious agencies have grown, multiplied, and taken on increasing importance in shaping and carrying people's religious identity."[6] Carpenter underscores the irony in this situation. Having been forced by the Protestant denominational establishment to move to the margins in order to survive, the fundamentalists promoted ways for Christians to associate with each other that went beyond the denominational structures. In doing so, they guaranteed their own survival by initiating "a trend that has led to the weakening of the most central and powerful corporate expressions of American religion."[7]

Some very healthy evangelical organizations today—many colleges and seminaries, mission and relief agencies, evangelistic associations, youth ministries, radio and television programs—owe their contemporary vitality to the organizational savvy of the earlier fundamentalist movement. This is certainly true of Fuller Seminary, the school over which Edward John Carnell had presided during the time he was formulating the basics of his attack on fundamentalism. The seminary had been founded in 1947 by Charles E. Fuller, an important pioneer in the field of religious broadcasting. While one of the gentler fundamentalist leaders, Dr. Fuller's successes in his international radio ministry—and in the founding of his seminary—are unthinkable apart from the vast organizational infrastructure fundamentalism had created.

A Healthy Remembering

Sigmund Freud, the founder of psychoanalysis, was fond of telling the story of a pastor who was summoned to the bedside of a dying insurance agent. The man was a professed atheist, but his family was hopeful that he might be open to the Christian message as he faced his own demise. The family members waited outside the room as the pastor and the insurance agent talked together. The conversation went on for a long time, and the family began to nurture the hope that a religious conversion was in process. When the door finally opened and the pastor emerged, however, they discovered that the dying insurance agent had remained in his unconverted state—but the pastor had been sold a new insurance policy!

Freud's primary intention in telling this story was to warn psychoanalysts not to compromise their principles. But it can also be used to illustrate some important questions about the present condition of evangelicalism. In rejecting the very real defects of fundamentalism during the past few decades, evangelicals have begun to take very seriously their responsibilities to the larger culture— and with some obvious signs of success. The questions we must face honestly are these: Have we sold a new policy to the culture— or has the culture sold us a policy?

There is no ignoring the fact that we are in a different cultural position from the days when our spiritual forebears spread sawdust on the ground in their revival tents. We certainly have a much friendlier relationship with our surroundings. Some commentators say we have actually *become* the "mainline" of Protestantism. Evangelicals can be found in positions of leadership in politics, the universities, the entertainment business, and the marketplace. Pentecostal and Holiness congregations, which once stood on the wrong side of the tracks, are now often-flourishing ecclesiastical enterprises occupying the best real estate in town. Yet the question must be asked: Have we lost some important spiritual sensitivities while all of this has been happening?

There is an interesting parallel between the social pilgrimage of evangelicals and that of Roman Catholics in this century. In the course of only one or two generations, American Catholics have gone from being a marginal immigrant community to a significant cultural presence in the United States. A number of commentators have observed that these changes have not been accompanied by a comparable shift in theological self-understanding. Many Catholic laypeople, for example, occupy significant leadership roles in American culture, but they were educated in a religious system that presupposed the need to "keep the faith" as immigrant communities rather than to take up the challenge of exercising power in the structures of the larger culture.

Similar things, I am convinced, can be said about evangelicals—and not only about our upwardly mobile laity but about our upwardly mobile clergy leaders as well. In the past we evangelical Protestants became accustomed to thinking of ourselves as a beleaguered remnant. We devoted much energy to preserving the integrity of our faith in what we saw as a hostile environment. And the kind of theology we heard in sermons and read in magazines was designed to reinforce this sense that we are destined to be a people who are on the margins of cultural life. We don't really belong in this world, we told ourselves. We are on our way to heaven's glory. The most important thing is to make it through by being faithful to the gospel and—as much as possible—without getting contaminated by our sinful surroundings.

We don't usually hear the case being made in such stark terms these days. We have a lot less to feel alienated about than we did in the past. Let me make it clear that I do not think this is necessarily a bad thing. I have expended considerable energy joining my voice with those who have called for an evangelical witness that speaks more credibly to the larger culture without losing the movement's distinctive strengths, and I do not think this effort has been misguided. Indeed, I occasionally complain that some of the defects that led to the marginalized mentality in the past still linger on in the evangelical community.

Unlike those evangelical thinkers who worry that our successes have inevitably weakened us spiritually and theologically, my
own inclination is to see the social gains of contemporary evangelicalism as presenting us with new opportunities for faithfulness.
And I see many evangelicals responding creatively to these challenges. I talk with seminary students on a daily basis who care
deeply about the cause of the gospel. I often hear "megachurch"
pastors boldly proclaiming the themes of sin, guilt, and redemption
through the blood of Jesus Christ. So, I am not discouraged about
the evangelical movement. But I do want us to think carefully
about who we are and what God calls us to be.

I am especially impressed these days with the importance of
historical mindfulness. The call issued by sociologist Robert Bellah
and his colleagues in *Habits of the Heart*—that churches and syn-
agogues must work hard at being "communities of memory" in a
culture fast losing its awareness of the past—is a poignant one for
evangelicals.

Indeed, memory loss was one of fundamentalism's biggest
defects. The fundamentalist movement often seemed to think that
the history of the "real" church jumped from the early church to a
quick stop at Martin Luther and then on to the fundamentalist-
modernist controversies of the early twentieth century. The Pentecostal and Holiness movements had their own versions of that kind
of abbreviated narrative of the Spirit's dealings with the church.
Traces of this kind of spiritual and theological amnesia can still
be detected in the evangelical movement.

A few years ago I met with a group of pastors from very large
"charismatic" churches. Each of their congregations numbered in
the thousands—many were conducting four and five services each
weekend. I tried to impress on them the importance of theological
education for pastors. Several of them made it clear they found
what I was saying quite unconvincing. "We're in the business of

getting people to come to church," they said; "seminaries are no help at all in telling us how to do that." I responded by admitting that while seminaries could do a better job in helping to promote this cause, we also are concerned about what people *learn* when we get them into a church. And for this we need pastors who are firmly grounded in biblical teaching, theological reflection, and a clear understanding of the history of God's dealings with the church. None of this seemed very attractive to this group of pastors. One of them did say, however, that there probably *is* some value in studying the history of past revivals in the Christian community.

The study of the history of revivals is, of course, a worthy project. But I'm also interested in looking at the forces that were at work to make revivals necessary. One obvious factor in bringing about spiritual decline is bad theology. If we fail to engage in the careful study of *ideas* in Christian history—worthy and unworthy ideas about God and his relationship to human beings—we run the real risk of constantly recycling old heresies.

A Pentecostal friend of mine once shared an interesting account of the ways in which the Assemblies of God have had to deal with various heretical views about faith healing during the twentieth century. A key biblical text for Pentecostalism's understanding of this topic has been Isaiah 53:5 (King James Version): "with his stripes we are healed." The standard Pentecostal interpretation of this verse has been that physical healing is *included* in the atoning work of Jesus Christ, so that we can expect on occasion miraculous displays of God's healing power in our bodies. This interpretation was an important corrective emphasis for the whole evangelical movement. But at times in the Assemblies of God certain people have taught that physical healing is *guaranteed* by the atonement, so that Christians can expect miraculous healings as a normal course of events in their lives. The denomination has regularly warned against this teaching. At other times, though, an even more radical notion has surfaced, namely, that physical healing is *accomplished* by the atoning work of Christ, so that if a person thinks she has a cold she is being deceived by Satan—with Christ's stripes she *is* healed! This teaching has also been rejected as heretical.

This history shows us that there resides in the Assemblies of God a collective wisdom about faith healing; contemporary Pentecostals and charismatics ignore this wisdom at their peril. And these are only a few of the lessons that the study of the Christian history can teach us. If we fail to be historically mindful, we run the risk of constantly recycling old heresies.

I find it necessary for my own spiritual well-being to remember the history of the fundamentalist movement in particular. I was surrounded in my youth by people for whom painful memories of spiritual and theological battles were still very vivid. Many of them had left denominations and had been evicted from church buildings where they had served faithfully. They had seen schools and agencies they loved come under the influence of strange theological teachings. They had experienced the loss of "goods and kindred"[8] because they refused to compromise their convictions.

I certainly entertain no illusion that the stories of their struggles were inerrant in all details. Nor do I deem it healthy to nurture past hurts in such a way that I insist on waging battles that no longer need to be fought. David Hubbard, the late president of Fuller Seminary, had a nice way of making this point. He said we evangelicals should look at the battles fought by previous generations in much the same way that American citizens honor the memories of those who fought in the Revolutionary War. "I can go to Bunker Hill," he said, "and feel patriotic, even though I have no animosity toward the present-day British."

Dr. Hubbard's image is an instructive one. Clearly it is important to remember our spiritual ancestors and to learn from their strengths and their weaknesses. But we do remember them as *ancestors*, as people who attempted to be faithful under conditions very different from our own context. We contemporary evangelicals must continue to visit our Bunker Hills. But the point of those visits is not to live in the past but to find new ways of engaging the present, knowing that to do so will require us to work together with—and learn important lessons from—Christian fellow travelers who regularly take their own detours, visiting very different shrines.

CHAPTER SEVEN

E M P H A S I Z I N G
F U N D A M E N T A L S

I believe in the "fundamentals"—those basic doctrines the fundamentalists insisted were nonnegotiable as they argued with modernists in the beginning decades of the twentieth century. The Virgin Birth of Jesus, his full divinity, the blood sacrifice character of his atoning work, the real physical body that came out of the tomb on Easter morning, the blessed hope of his Second Coming—these are items of faith I profess without reservation.

When my friends from other Christian traditions—for example, Roman Catholic or Eastern Orthodox—ask me why I call myself an evangelical, I usually give them a brief history of the fundamentalist-modernist disputes, and then I tell them about the later "neo-evangelical" movement. Along the way I provide them with a list of the "fundamentals." Their responses are often perplexed ones. Why this particular list? These doctrines do not add up to a very robust theological perspective! Why is it, for example, that no mention is made of anything about the church, or anything about the sacraments?

My honest answer is that of course the list of things we typically emphasize does not come close to comprising a comprehensive theological perspective when compared to classical confessional traditions. And, I admit, it is regrettable that large numbers of evangelicals—and not only those of the fundamentalist variety—do in fact operate with an extremely limited theological perspective.

In all fairness, it needs to be recognized that many fundamentalists have a rather detailed theology of the sacraments—or, as most of them would prefer to say, of "ordinances." The "closed" Plymouth Brethren, for example, who are known for their strict separatism and (often) their strong commitment to dispensationalist teaching, have made the Lord's Supper a central feature of their worshiping life. And most fundamentalists have a detailed theology of "believers' baptism"; some even have rather strong views about the proper mode of baptism.

A Modifying Label

For all of that, though, I do not see evangelicalism as generating a very rich theological system. And for this reason I am not happy when people treat "fundamentalism" and "evangelicalism" as labels that refer to theological perspectives in the same way as "Lutheranism" and "Orthodox" do. I think "evangelical" is best thought of as a theological modifier rather than as a noun. The label should not be allowed to stand alone when sorting out theological systems.

The key features of evangelical thought are best seen as theological *emphases* that have come to have importance in the context of certain kinds of theological struggles. This is, I suggest, the best way of understanding "the fundamentals." One reason I believe in the literal virgin birth of Jesus is simply because I see it to be clearly taught in the New Testament. But this belief takes on a special significance for me, and for other evangelicals, because it is one of those biblical teachings that liberals make a point of denying. They insist, for example, that the early Christians began to tell this story of Jesus' birth in order to highlight the special status of Jesus as a teacher who was uniquely "sent by God." We evangelicals see a deeper issue at stake here. The basic question is whether we are willing to accept the worldview of the Bible. The God who created the world out of nothing by the word of his power is the same God who called forth the decomposing body of Jesus from the tomb. And he is the same God who planted new life in the womb of Mary without the agency of a human father.

What makes the "fundamentals" important for evangelicals, then, is their role in the very real struggles in which we have been involved. Beliefs about what happens in the Lord's Supper, or how we spell out our understanding of the Trinity, or whether justification precedes or follows regeneration in "the order of salvation"—these too are important topics. But they have not been important in the most wrenching theological controversies that have shaped evangelicalism as a movement. And that is why our favorite theological emphases do not by themselves comprise a rich theological system.

In order to provide an accurate identification of my own theological position I find it necessary to say I am an "evangelical Calvinist." I take the "Calvinist" part of this very seriously. In addition to endorsing the views about salvation set forth by John Calvin in his *Institutes of the Christian Religion* and developed further in the confessions and catechisms of the sixteenth and seventeenth centuries, I also adhere to the Reformed tradition's perspectives on the church and the sacraments. And like other people in this tradition, my theology draws heavily on the views set forth in, say, the creeds adopted at Nicea and Chalcedon. I judge that this affinity provides me with a fairly robust theological perspective, one that leads me into interesting debates with persons who use the term "evangelical" to modify other theological perspectives—Wesleyan or Anabaptist or Lutheran, for example.

But the "evangelical" modifier itself is also important to my understanding of my theological identity. It means, for one thing, that as a good pietist I will worry about certain kinds of scholastic tendencies in some branches of Reformed orthodoxy. And it also means that I will be inclined to warn against both modernist and postmodernist revisionisms in the mainline Presbyterian denomination to which I belong. And it means that, while I enjoy debating points of theology with those who attach the "evangelical" label to other confessional perspectives, I also see myself as being united with them in the common cause of celebrating the witness of those in the past who have risked much in defending a very specific set of "fundamentals."

The Fundamentalist "Order"

My rather lengthy exposure to fundamentalism has not left me badly bruised. Indeed, I am basically grateful for the experience. But I know many people whose stories are different from mine. They were deeply hurt by fundamentalism. When they tell me about what happened to them, I listen with genuine sympathy.

I met a woman who told me the long and painful story about how she came to reject her fundamentalist upbringing. The rejection is so complete for her that she does not even like the "evangelical" label. She wants to get as far away as she can from what she calls "the legalism and separatism" of that kind of Christianity. And she has found a safe refuge in the Episcopal church. "Anglicanism has taught me to have a positive attitude toward the world in which I live," she reported. "It has given me a sacramental view of reality." Regularly participating in the Eucharist is now the most important thing in her life. She also goes on regular spiritual retreats. She visits a Benedictine monastery and spends much time in silence. She likes to be around the monks. She says they inspire her to pursue a deeper spirituality.

I listened carefully to her testimony, and I told her I was really glad she has found a spiritual home where she can feel safe. And I meant it. I had no desire to argue with her or to encourage her to look in different places for her spiritual nurture.

It was the part about monks, though, that got me thinking later on about the parallels between monasticism and fundamentalism. This Christian woman dislikes fundamentalism because it had taught her to separate herself from "the world." But it is also the kind of thing monks have adopted as a way of life. And "all those rules" she despises about fundamentalism—well, monks too follow a Rule, and a pretty strict one at that.

I'm pretty sure I know how she would respond if I pointed out these things to her. She would tell me the separatism and legalism of the monks are different sorts of things from the patterns of fundamentalism. Monks don't insist everyone has to live the way they do. They don't have children whose lives they make miserable. A monk senses a unique call from God to the separated life. The monastic way is a "special vocation."

She would be right to tell me these things. The real problem with fundamentalists is not that they want to live by many rules that keep them separate from "worldliness"; it's that they insist that *anyone* who wants to be a Christian should live this way. They don't see their ways of obeying God as a "special vocation." For them the fundamentalist way is simply the normal way of pleasing God. Anyone who sees things differently is in big trouble.

Again, this is the right way to see the difference between the separatism and legalism of fundamentalism and that of the monastic way. But, having acknowledged the point, I still find the parallel to be fascinating. It has helped me to understand a bit better why I continue to have a deep appreciation for the fundamentalists who influenced me in positive ways in my past, even though I no longer subscribe to their legalism and separatism. I see those fundamentalists as members of a special religious "order."

Members of religious orders—monks, for example—take special vows. They promise never to have sexual intercourse, and not to wear fancy clothes, and not to spend a lot of money on gourmet meals. In doing so, they are not saying that everyone should take those vows. They do so because they want to serve God in special ways. And the rest of us—those who do get married and shop for fashionable clothes and occasionally treat ourselves to meals in expensive restaurants—we can look to these monks as models of a special kind of faithfulness, even though we do not attempt to be faithful in the same ways.

And that's how I also see the fundamentalists whom I admire. I think of them as a kind of religious order whose members have taken special vows. Of course, I know they would not explain their commitments in that way. But I choose to admire them *as if* they were doing these things because of a "special vocation." It helps me make sense of the way they attempt to serve the Lord. I think it also illuminates the role they can play in the larger Christian community. And it helps me understand why I continue to draw spiritual strength from their example—even though I have taken some very different vows!

CHAPTER EIGHT

TO THE JEW FIRST

When a reporter for the Jewish Telegraphic Agency wrote a story about me in August of 1997, she portrayed me as "a conflicted man."[1] Our conversation together had been fairly cordial. She knew I had drawn some criticism for cosponsoring a conference on Fuller's campus with the American Jewish Committee. The conference focused on the ways in which religious people attempt to influence public life, which should have been a fairly tame topic. But in arranging the conference the Jewish planners made it clear they were nervous about the presence of a sizable group of messianic Jews at Fuller. I had insisted that these Jewish converts to Christianity be encouraged to attend our sessions—otherwise there could be no conference.

My Jewish friends reluctantly agreed, but they weren't the only ones who were nervous about the arrangement. Messianic Jews have long resented the ways in which they are shunned by the Jewish community, and many of them worried that I had forged an unhealthy compromise. It looked to them like they were being allowed into the discussion only under the assumption that they would be willing to be a part of a bland "dialogue," where important issues between traditional Jews and Jewish followers of Christ would be set aside as irrelevant—thus giving the impression that Fuller was backing off from a commitment to Jewish evangelism. Ironically, some constituents of the American Jewish Committee had the opposite worry: They feared that by agreeing to meet on a seminary campus known for its commitment to Jews for Jesus and similar groups, the Jewish community would be implicitly endorsing the legitimacy of Jewish evangelism.

When I talked with the reporter from the Jewish Telegraphic Agency, I told her I was willing to live with these tensions. We evangelicals are indeed committed to Jewish evangelism. But we also need to be in dialogue with the larger Jewish community about important matters of common interest. This is why she portrayed me as "a conflicted man" on the subject of evangelical-Jewish relations. The president of Fuller Seminary, she wrote, is "torn between fealty to his faith, which requires him to proselytize 'the Jew first,' and his desire to respect all religious people." To reinforce her point, she quoted a well-known rabbi with whom I have worked on several projects dealing with religion in public life. Acknowledging our friendship, the rabbi offered the opinion that I am caught up in "the irreconcilable tension which is so much a part of evangelical-Jewish relations, and between his faith commitment and his commitment toward Jews and society." But he also told the reporter that there is hope for me. I am, he said, "a religious pilgrim" who may eventually come to a more consistent position on the subject.

These Jewish commentators have me pretty much figured out. I am indeed firmly committed to Jewish evangelism—a fact they understandably find disturbing. And I do also have a deep respect for the Jewish people. And there is indeed a kind of "irreconcilable tension" in trying to hold this all together. I hope the rabbi is right—that someday I will hold a more consistent position on the subject. In the meantime I have chosen to live with the tension.

Israel: "Old" and "New"

Actually, the tension I experience in this area is rooted in some continuing *theological* puzzles I regularly think about. How are we as New Testament Christians to understand the theological status of Jewishness in our present context?

For a while in my life I tried hard to get rid of the puzzle by trying out—indeed, by *defending* in some of my writings—what seemed to me to be a straightforward theological position, a fairly standard one for Reformed Christians, especially as they attempt to provide a coherent alternative to dispensationalist teaching. The position rests on this basic theological move: to treat God's special attitude of favor toward Israel in the Old Testament as now being completely transferred to the New Testament church.

There is much to be said for making this move. The church is, after all, in an important sense "the new Israel." In my thinking about this theme I have been especially taken with the imagery employed in the First Epistle of Peter. The apostle is writing to a group of Christians that obviously includes Gentiles, but he begins his letter with Old Testament terminology, greeting his readers as "the exiles of the Dispersion" (1 Peter 1:1 New Revised Standard Version). Especially significant is the way, in the second chapter, he takes a series of images of Old Testament Israel and now applies them to the New Testament church: "But you are a chosen race, a royal priesthood, a holy nation, God's own people," adding a quotation from one of the prophets: "Once you were not a people, but now you are God's people" (1 Peter 2:9–10 New Revised Standard Version).

These have been significant verses to help clarify my own thinking about the nature of Christian community. At the Bible conference where I worked in my teenage years, I heard a fundamentalist preacher argue that Satan always promises unity, and that in our own day the devil was actively promoting "one world race, one world church, and one world government." This meant, he insisted, that all true Bible-believing Christians must oppose the racial desegregation movement, the World Council of Churches, and the United Nations. I remember feeling at the time that this view, even though it tied a lot of issues together in a neat package, was nonetheless a troubling one. I had no strong views about ecumenism or international relations, but I had been a Brooklyn Dodgers fan, and Jackie Robinson was my hero—I was thrilled by his courage as he overcame prejudice in desegregating major league baseball, and I had a hard time thinking of him as a tool of Satan!

I gradually came to reject the whole picture set forth by that preacher. But I was never completely clear about how unbiblical his viewpoint was until I realized the implications of 1 Peter 2:9–10. God is putting together a new kind of "race," a new kind of "priesthood," and a new kind of "nation." Jesus is in the business of actively promoting unity. He does not want us to define ourselves along artificial lines of what the sinful world sees as ethnic-racial or denominational or national identities. Through the blood of Jesus Christ we have been made into a new kind of people, in which "there is neither Jew nor Greek, slave nor free, male nor female, for you are all one in Christ Jesus" (Galatians 3:28). Here the idea of the church as a new kind of "Israel" was a compelling image.

Finding "Israel" Today

Again, this way of viewing things has been constructive for my understanding of the nature of the church—and indeed of the basis for Christian social ethics. But I realize now that I have often put the underlying theological point in too unqualified a manner.

Once I gave a speech, for example, on the topic "Where Is Israel Today?" I began by explaining my question. I wanted to understand where we will find that group of people in contemporary life who are the present-day intended beneficiaries of the promises God made to Israel in Old Testament times. Then I explained what I took to be two mistaken answers Christians often give to my question.

The first answer is that the contemporary beneficiary of those promises is, simply, flesh-and-blood Israel—the present-day Jewish people. This, I explained, is the viewpoint of dispensational theology. To illustrate the point, I quoted Lewis Sperry Chafer's statement that we must never confuse "God's consistent and eternal earthly purposes, which is the substance of Judaism, and His consistent and eternal heavenly purpose, which is the substance of Christianity."[2] On this view, God's ancient promises to the Jewish people are still in effect. The Lord wants them to be a flourishing nation, and he has brought them back to their original homeland where, in fulfillment of prophecy, they will someday acknowledge Jesus as the true Messiah of Israel.

The second answer is that of civil religion. I pointed out the deeply entrenched pattern in the United States of seeing the American people as comprising "a chosen people." Jonathan Edwards, for one, had been very explicit in setting forth this case. Many of the Old Testament prophecies were now being fulfilled, he said, in North America. He singled out Isaiah 60 (verses 1, 3, and 5), with its vision of a glorified Jerusalem, as especially relevant in this regard:

> Arise, shine, for your light has come, and the glory of the LORD rises upon you.... Nations will come to your light, and kings to the brightness of your dawn.... the wealth on the seas will be brought to you, to you the riches of the nations will come.

I also talked about how I saw this theme influencing our foreign policy—where we often acted as if we were a nation with a messianic mission in the world.

I rejected these two answers and set forth a third as the only proper way to understand who "Israel" is today: The church of Jesus Christ is the new Israel. All of the basic promises of divine favor God made to the Jews in the Old Testament are now directed toward that blood-bought community drawn "from every tribe and language and people and nation" and formed by sovereign grace into a new kind of "kingdom and priests to serve our God" (Revelation 5:9–10).

Living with the Mystery

I am no longer content with the starkness of this way of spelling things out. To be sure, I still do not have any sympathy for the way in which civil religion selectively adapts Old Testament themes to undergird a superpatriotism. But I cannot simply reject the notion of a continuing attitude of divine favor for the Jewish people in the way I once did—even though I continue to make much good use of the idea that the church has also been incorporated, in an important sense, into a new and expanded version of the old Israel.

The only failing grade I ever received for a course during my years in school was while I was a seminary student. The course was on the Epistle to the Romans, and much of the grade was based on the writing of a ten-page exegetical paper. I chose to write on Romans 11, where the apostle discusses the theological status of the Jews since the coming of Christ. I eagerly set about to complete the assignment, reading commentators who set forth a variety of interpretations. I also worked through the chapter in the Greek language, reading it over many times.

I never wrote the paper, and my "Incomplete" became an "F" on my record. It is one of the few times in my life when I simply could not put my thoughts on paper. The more I read the apostle Paul on the subject, the more I was convinced he was not setting forth a clear step-by-step case for a coherent perspective on the subject. This awareness was deeply distressing for me. I *wanted* him to be absolutely clear about the status of the Jews. I was committed to being orthodox in my theology, and I had no room for messiness in what I saw as the Bible's teaching on an important topic. Furthermore, I was studying in a Reformed seminary, and I was eager to demonstrate that the promises associated with God's old covenant with ethnic Israel have now been transferred to the church of Jesus Christ, the people of the new covenant. But I did not know how to make the case confidently, so I never wrote the paper.

In subsequent years I developed my views about the church as the new Israel as a basis for Christian social ethics. In doing so, as I have already reported, I made much use of Peter's First Epistle and other passages that gave support to such a view. But I always had a nagging sense I was cheating a bit—that I had no right to state my case so boldly unless I could make my peace with Romans 11.

Well, I have made my peace—after a fashion, that is. I can now read Romans 11 with a quiet conscience because I have learned how to live with some messiness in my theology. I do not see the apostle Paul as making a perfectly coherent case on the subject of the Jews. He goes back and forth: Their rejection of Jesus as the heaven-sent Messiah is seriously displeasing to God; they are branches that have been broken off, and a wild shoot has been grafted in their place (see Romans 11:17), but Gentiles should not take this as a cause for pride, since the Jews are still the "natural branches" who will eventually be grafted back into the tree (11:25). Does this mean, then, that Israel as a people will be saved? Well, "God has bound all men over to disobedience so that he may have mercy on them all" (11:32). Having read Paul thus far on the subject, I want desperately to have him answer a few more important questions for clarification, since I cannot put all of this together into a coherent package. But instead he starts singing a hymn about the mystery of God's ways. And I have learned at this stage of my theological journey to set aside my questions and simply sing along with Paul:

> Oh, the depth of the riches of the wisdom and
>   knowledge of God!
>   How unsearchable his judgments,
>   and his paths beyond tracing out!
> "Who has known the mind of the Lord?
>   Or who has been his counselor?"
> "Who has ever given to God,
>   that God should repay him?"
> For from him and through him and to him are all things.
>   To him be the glory forever!
>   Amen.
>
> ROMANS 11:33–36

Assessing Dispensationalism

Looking back on my experience of not being able to write my paper for my seminary class, I can see now I was trying too hard not to side with dispensationalism in its insistence on the continuing special status of the Jews in God's dealings with humankind. I can now allow myself to experience some gratitude to dispensationalists for influencing me on this topic. They gave me a disposition to wrestle with some significant questions, some of which have great practical importance for the life of the church of Jesus Christ in today's world. At the same time, it is on many of the practical issues that I find dispensationalism to be especially unhelpful—even an obstacle at times that stands in the way of clear thinking about the church's mission.

I am especially disturbed by what I see as a refusal on the part of many dispensationalists to criticize the policies of Israeli governments. A few years ago I met with an Arab Christian from the Middle East who was visiting our campus. We talked together about the challenges facing the churches in general and theological educators in particular in her part of the world. I asked her a question I regularly pose to international visitors: "What are the theological issues the folks back home really get excited about?" Without a moment's hesitation she responded: "Whether we can preach from the Old Testament! When the worshipers in our churches hear the stories about Israel as God's chosen people, it is very upsetting, given the way the present-day Israelis have brought such destruction into our lives."

Christians in Arab countries have some good reasons to resent the policies of Israeli governments. Unfortunately, dispensationalists often obscure these issues. They are often so caught up in an enthusiasm for "Bible prophecy" scenarios that they take it as obligatory to support the Israeli cause no matter what. They see any opposition to Israel's policies to be an attempt to thwart God's purposes in history. I find this posture to be unbiblical—even on dispensationalist premises. Suppose that the establishment of the modern state of Israel is indeed a fulfillment of prophecy. And suppose God wants Israel to prosper in the land, in preparation for the day when the Jewish people will acknowledge Christ as the promised Messiah. None of this exempts us from assessing, and criticizing when necessary, the details of Israeli policies. The Old Testament prophets make it clear that the nation of Israel will never be truly blessed by God unless she pursues justice. To want present-day Israel to flourish as a nation is to want her to treat her citizens—and her neighbors—justly. We are not on the side of God's plan for Israel if we refuse to subject her actions to critical scrutiny in the light of revealed norms for what it means for a nation to please the Lord.

I also worry much about the failure of dispensationlists to take a strong stand against anti-Semitism. Some scholars have even detected a strain of anti-Semitism in the dispensationalist movement. At first glance this may seem odd for a school of thought that places such a singular emphasis on God's eternal commitment to the Jewish people. But dispensationalists often direct their affection toward an idealized Judaism. They support an *abstract version* of a divine "plan" for the Jews more than they support individual Jewish people. At the very least, their theology of Judaism has not regularly manifested itself in active efforts to eradicate anti-Semitism. And it is precisely in this area—the very real presence of anti-Semitism in modern life—where my own concerns about evangelical-Jewish relations are especially focused.

What's more, I'm somewhat worried about how dispensationalist attitudes toward Jewishness can cloud our understanding of the status of ethnicity as such in the divine plan for humankind. It is certainly undeniable that in ancient times God chose to bestow special favors on a specific ethnic people. Because of the idolatrous project that took place at Babel (see Genesis 11:1–9), God chose to accomplish his redemptive purposes by singling out a specific ethnic-cultural group, the Hebrew nation, as the special recipient of his covenant mercies. In that sense, salvation was closely tied to a specific ethnic identity in the Old Testament: To be identified with "the people of God," it was necessary either to be born a Jew or otherwise incorporated into the Jewish community. But this ethnocentric redemptive economy of the old covenant was never viewed—contrary to what I was taught by dispensationalists—as the final arrangement. The prophets of Israel, inspired by the Spirit of God, looked forward to something greater that would someday happen: "On this mountain the LORD Almighty will prepare a feast of rich food for all peoples.... On this mountain he will destroy the shroud that enfolds all peoples, the sheet that covers all nations" (Isaiah

25:6-7); "It is too small a thing for you to be my servant to restore the tribes of Jacob and bring back those of Israel I have kept. I will also make you a light for the Gentiles, that you may bring my salvation to the ends of the earth" (Isaiah 49:6).

This promise was realized in a very dramatic way on the day of Pentecost, when the curse of Babel was reversed through the power of the Holy Spirit (see Acts 2). The post-Pentecost church is now called to show forth a new kind of social reality, in which older ethnic identities are subordinated to the new cultural patterns that come with life in the Spirit. This church in its present life and witness is called to point forward to the sanctified multiculturalism that will be celebrated before the heavenly throne as people from many tribes and languages and peoples and nations will sing praises to the Lamb (see Revelation 5:9; 7:9-17).

I must quickly add that this does not rule out the acknowledgment that God still honors a continuing commitment to the specific ethnic people who served as his special agent under the older covenant. But this commitment is to a people who, already in ancient times, were encouraged to anticipate a day when God's Spirit would be poured out on all flesh (see Numbers 11:29; Joel 2:28). There was never a time when the Israel of God had a right to think the covenant blessings were her exclusive property.

I think all of this means that God takes ethnicity very seriously. It may even be that we will in some important sense bring our ethnicities with us into that eschatological multitude no human being will be able to count (see Revelation 7:9). If so, we might have to think about the ways in which not only Israel, but all ethnic Christian groups, need both to celebrate and yet de-absolutize their "natural" identities as they realize together their larger identity as the blood-bought people of the Lamb.

These are extremely important issues in a day when we see vivid signs of the reality of Babel all around us. We have urgent reasons today to sort out our views about the relationship between Israel and the church in a way that will point to the great work of Pentecost so that we can anticipate in our present life and witness the future ingathering of the honor and the glory of the nations.

A Saint to Emulate

Every few years I reread Corrie ten Boom's wonderful book, *The Hiding Place*. While I never saw her in person, Corrie ten Boom is one of my special saints—a kind of Dutch grandmotherly, nurturing example of faithfulness. I draw much inspiration from the account of her efforts to protect Jewish people from the horrible designs of the Nazis. There can be no doubt that she wanted everyone—Jew and Gentile alike—to come to know Jesus. She knew the only truly safe "hiding place" was to be found in the Savior's embrace. But a desire to evangelize was not the sole motivation in her relations with Jews. She was willing to risk her life to work for their physical safety, even if those efforts did not afford opportunities to lead them to Christ.

An especially moving scene for me took place when her family first became directly aware of the horrible things the Nazis were doing to the Jews. The ten Booms had begun to see Jews wearing the required yellow stars and were hearing stories of mysterious disappearances. But one day as Corrie and her father were walking along a street in Haarlem, they noticed that the entire market area had been cordoned off. When they stopped to see what was happening, they observed Jewish men, women, and children being forced into trucks by the German soldiers. "Father! Those poor people!" Corrie cried out. "Those poor people," echoed her father. But when Corrie looked at Father ten Boom's face, she saw that he was staring, not at the Jews, but at the Nazis. "I pity the poor Germans, Corrie," he said. "They have touched the apple of God's eye."[3]

I find this both inspiring and theologically intriguing. I wonder what specific theological views about Judaism influenced the ten Boom family. Perhaps they were familiar with dispensationalist teachings. But it is also quite possible they were drawing on themes present in the Dutch Reformed tradition. In the North American Dutch Reformed community, conservative Reformed theologians often argue strenuously against any continuation of God's special covenant promises to the Jews—along lines similar to the version of "the-church-as-the-new-Israel" I have defended in the past. But I have detected a different theological emphasis among Reformed thinkers in the Netherlands, who otherwise operate with a theological perspective resembling that of their American counterparts.

I once asked a person who had worked in the Dutch underground during the Nazi occupation about his theological perspective. He was a devout Calvinist layman who immigrated to the United States after the war. He spoke with deep emotion about specific Jews who had found a hiding place in his home and in the homes of his neighbors. I asked him: "How in the light of the Bible do you understand your relationship to Jewish people?" His reply surprised me: "I think it is more of a psychological thing. We Dutch Reformed types place such a strong emphasis on our being 'in the covenant' that on an emotional level we sort of feel a strong kinship with the Jews." Then he chuckled: "I guess it's because we both think of ourselves as God's elect people! Our destinies are intertwined!"

Thinking about his comment later, I came to the conclusion that his perspective wasn't *simply* "a psychological thing." He was also talking theology. Strong kinship. Election. Intertwined destinies. Those are theological themes—*mysterious* theological themes, the kind that if you take them seriously you end up with a little messiness in your theology. A messiness that, in turn, might lead a Jewish reporter to describe you as "a conflicted person."

A Threefold Agenda

Much of my conflictedness about my relationship with Jewish people, however, has to do with a sense of being out of step with some prominent patterns of thinking on the subject—patterns that seem to me to border on reductionism. I have a nonnegotiable commitment to evangelism—and this includes witnessing to Jewish people about my firm conviction that Jesus is the promised Messiah. But I also oppose treating Jews as though they were only "targets" for evangelism. We evangelicals have much to learn from Jews about issues of public life and also about deeply religious topics. And we must work alongside members of the Jewish community in striving for justice and righteousness in the larger society.

Witnessing to; learning from; cooperating with—this seems to me to be an important threefold Christian agenda for our relationships with the Jewish community. But there don't seem to be many Christians who are willing to endorse the whole agenda. Those who have been strong on evangelism have often been weak on learning and cooperation; those who have been eager to nurture learning and cooperative relationships have often downplayed the evangelistic mandate.

Let's be clear about this: Evangelism *is* a mandate. The Southern Baptists took considerable criticism a few years ago for their announcement about a program in Jewish evangelism, and I hope this controversy will at least serve to inform the larger world that some of us really do believe we have an obligation to present the claims of Christ to non-Christians. We evangelicals need to keep reminding our Jewish friends that if they are really serious about having better relations with us—and I sense many Jews are indeed serious in this intention—they cannot demand that we think and act like liberal Protestants or Roman Catholics. This is a price of admission we cannot pay. We are *evangel* people. Our proclamation that Jesus is the promised Messiah cannot be silenced for the sake of interreligious civility.

But faithfulness to the gospel also requires *more* than evangelism. We have much to learn from the Jewish people. For one thing, our relationships with messianic Jews, as well as with other Jewish brothers and sisters who have come to faith in Christ, have been precious to many of us and have deepened our understanding of the gospel. But non-Christian Jews also have much to teach us about spiritual matters. Any Christian who thinks otherwise should read Abraham Joshua Heschel on the prophets or the Sabbath, or the fiction of Chaim Potok—or even Harry Kemelman's *Rabbi Small* mystery novels. We cannot simply classify Judaism under "Other Religions." We share with Jewish people a common spiritual heritage grounded in God's revelation to Moses and the Hebrew prophets.

Furthermore, we must also learn about the suffering of the Jewish people. Evangelicals need to think more deeply about what it means to evangelize Jews after the Holocaust (the period of time—1933–1945—in which Jewish men, women, and children were systematically eliminated by the Nazis). Much has happened in Jewish-Christian relations since the New Testament was written. Our Christian record in these two thousand years of history is not an admirable one. Indeed, we have often committed atrocious deeds against Jews. I will never forget the tears of a Jewish friend as he told me about his childhood in a predominantly Christian town in the Midwest, when his classmates taunted him by chanting "Christ-killer" as they followed him home from school.

Evangelical Christians need to weep with Jews as we hear the stories of their suffering. And we must repent of our sins, even as we testify about the One who came to save us while we were still sinners (see Romans 5:8). We cannot simply quote Pauline passages—written when the church was a minority religion struggling

to clarify both continuities and differences with a Jewish majority—without recognizing we are doing so from this side of
Auschwitz. When Jews, both religious and secular, complain that
our evangelistic efforts threaten to destroy their very identity as a
people, we must listen carefully. And we must recognize that our
responses—however theologically appropriate they may be from a
Christian perspective—will not be very convincing to people who
have vivid collective memories of forced "conversions." None of this
cancels our obligation to evangelize, but it does highlight our obligation to avoid unnecessary offense and to be clear about the challenges we face.

And we must cooperate with Jews in the larger task of working for the health of society. One obvious threat to justice today
was described succinctly several years ago when the Lausanne Con-
sultation on Jewish Evangelism denounced the "proliferation of
racism and Jew-hatred in our world today"; this concern should
rank high on the agenda for evangelical-Jewish cooperation. We can
also work together in seeking creative resolutions to conflicts in
the Middle East. Evangelicals in the United States have a special
obligation to show by our deeds that we are committed to a plu-
ralistic society. Our regular references to America's identity as "a
Christian nation," however well-intentioned in the context of our
debates with secularists, are hurtful in the context of our relationship with Judaism. We need to demonstrate that we are willing to work with Jews and others as "co-belligerents"—to use one
of Christian apologist Francis Schaeffer's favorite terms—in finding a common moral basis for promoting the good order of our plu-
ralistic society.

Dialogue and cooperation with Jews have their own genuine
value. They should not be construed as mere "setups" for evangelism. But the connections to Christian witness are also very real.
In essence evangelism is witnessing to the marvelous message of

the God who has drawn near to us in Jesus Christ. If we want to tell of the power of the gospel "to the Jew first" (Romans 1:16 New Revised Standard Version) in our contemporary context, we may need first of all to draw near to our Jewish friends in order to learn from them—and work with them—on matters that are of profound significance in our contemporary world.

CHAPTER NINE

DISPENSATIONALIST
BLESSINGS

I have a little more to say about dispensationalism—this time not about its understanding of God's relationship with the Jews but as a broader perspective on what is happening in the world. Evangelical scholars who criticize fundamentalism for what they view as its distortions and excesses often reserve a few especially harsh words for dispensationalist teaching. When Edward John Carnell launched his "neo-evangelical" attack on fundamentalism, he saw dispensationalism as an obvious manifestation of an "orthodoxy gone cultic." And more recently Professor Mark Noll, in his important book, *The Scandal of the Evangelical Mind,* singled out dispensationalism as one of the more scandalous factors contributing to evangelical anti-intellectualism. Some prominent dispensationalist themes have even taken a pounding in the past decade from people who have long identified themselves with the dispensationalist camp. Proponents of "progressive dispensationalism," several of them faculty members at Dallas Theological Seminary, are engaged these days in an extensive revisionist project.

While I see the point of the criticisms, I must admit to some mixed feelings about all of this. I have spent much of my adult life in theological circles where hostility toward dispensationalist thought often runs rampant. On occasion I have slipped into some of these patterns myself. But I have never been able to join the critics with a completely clear conscience, for I have experienced the spiritual and theological strengths of dispensationalism in a very personal way. My spiritual journey has never taken me very far from dispensationalist environs. Dispensationalist theology has had a profound impact on my life, and as a result it has always been difficult for me simply to accept the charge that dispensationalism is nothing more than a distorted way of reading the Scriptures. I have known too many saints who have drawn much strength for their lives of faithfulness to the gospel from a spiritual culture shaped by dispensationalist thought.

Predictive Prophesying

I was meeting with a very bright Fuller student as his mentor for a rather technical theological project in which he was engaged. The working part of our session was over. "Before you leave," I said, "tell me about your background. How did you get interested in this kind of study?" He told me he had become a Christian during his student days at a university—"a dramatic conversion," he said—and then he went on to explain how he had found his way to Fuller Seminary. When he finished the story, I asked him to go back to the part about the dramatic conversion: "How did it happen?"

He blushed a little. "I was hoping you wouldn't ask. But since you did, I'll tell you. I became a Christian through reading Hal Lindsey's *The Late Great Planet Earth*—not a very popular book at Fuller Seminary! I certainly don't read that kind of thing these days, but it was an important factor in bringing me to Christ. I saw this book in a bookstore, and I was fascinated by the idea that the Bible could tell you what is going to happen in the future. As I read the book, though, what really got to me was the need to come to know Christ personally. That's how I became a Christian!"

A few weeks later I was attending a gathering of theologians from various traditions. At one point someone made a snide comment about "the kind of pseudo-prophecy stuff you find in Hal Lindsey." Most of the other people nodded knowingly—but I did not. I breathed a silent prayer of thanks for Lindsey's role in bringing my student to Christ.

I have to confess, though, that such a prayer does not come easily for me. As I developed my own way of thinking biblically about current events, I thought of myself as shedding most of what is associated with "Bible prophecy teaching." Hal Lindsey's kind of predictive prophesying was rather standard fare in my youth. I have a vivid memory of an evangelist who came to town, announcing that at his first service he would preach on the subject "Are Hitler and Roosevelt Really Dead?" He was fairly certain they were still alive—Adolf Hitler's body was never found and Franklin D. Roosevelt's coffin was never opened for public viewing—and that the two of them were in South America plotting against the forces of righteousness. He backed up his speculations with abundant references to Scripture verses that dealt, as he saw it, with contemporary events. I don't remember the details, but I do recall his telling us that whenever the Bible refers to "Gomer" it means Germany and that Ezekiel's references to "the prince of Meshech" are pointing to somebody who is ruling in Moscow.

That kind of thinking, I later decided, was responsible for an unhealthy "scorecard" mentality among evangelicals. We were encouraged to think of ourselves as standing on the sidelines of the arena of history, passively watching prophetic scenarios unfold as we checked them off on lists we had been given by Bible prophecy experts. As a budding evangelical activist in the 1970s, I insisted that the healthy alternative is to see prophecy as not so much "foretelling" as "forthtelling"—we should, I insisted, spend less time

98 THE SMELL OF SAWDUST

looking for obscure predictions about the future in Daniel and Ezekiel and more time bearing witness to the message about God's justice proclaimed so clearly in Isaiah and Amos.

While I still see things this way, I do notice in retrospect some of the nuances in the rhetoric I employed in making my case. For example, in the last paragraph I did not describe myself as saying we should simply *replace* foretelling with forthtelling. Rather, I said we should spend less time with the former and more with the latter. I have never seen my way clear simply to distance myself from everything talked about by the Bible prophecy teachers. For example, I don't disagree with everything Hal Lindsey says about the future. What's more, I not only believe that Jesus is coming again, but I also take seriously the possibility that we are in those "last days" prophesied in the Scriptures, when wars and earthquakes and widespread lawlessness signal the imminent return of Jesus Christ. I also believe that while the spirit of "antichrist" has always been present in sinful human history, we must be on guard for the appearance of a very real and visible antichrist who will appear on the world stage as a great deceiver of humankind (see 2 Thessalonians 2:1–12; 1 John 2:18). And while I am inclined toward an "amillennial" position, I am regularly impressed by the plausibility of the view that a literal millennial reign by Christ is a part of the scenario for the wrapping up of human history as we know it. But I also recognize in myself a reluctance to talk about these things, in least in part out of a reaction against the excesses of the dispensationalists.

The student who had been converted by reading *The Late Great Planet Earth* assured me he no longer needed to dwell on the sort of detail provided in that book. But my sense is that he was drawn to Christ by a legitimate desire to face the future with some general knowledge about what will come to pass in the world. Hal Lindsey may have given him more information than he needed—

but I worry that a more cautious evangelicalism may err on the side of providing too *few* details.

Prophecy and Activism

At a 1972 conference at Wheaton College, I was asked to give the opening prayer at an evening lecture. I prayed for the person who would be giving the lecture, as well as for those of us who would be listening, that we might all advance in our understanding of an important topic. I concluded my prayer with words that went something like this: "And as we ask you, O Lord, to bless us here as we attempt to advance the cause of truth, we also pray for your blessing this night on all who work for the cause of peace and justice and righteousness in the world. Amen."

After the session a man came up to chide me. "I resented your pro-McGovern prayer!" he said. (The war in Vietnam was being fought, and George McGovern was running for president on an anti-war platform.) I was taken aback: "What in the world was 'pro-McGovern' about my prayer?" "You prayed for peace," he responded. "Don't you know there will be no peace in the world until the Prince of Peace returns?" He walked away.

I'm glad we didn't get into an argument, because I'm sure it would have gone badly. My instinct was to challenge his assumption that we have no hope for success in our peace-making efforts prior to Christ's return. But this argument wouldn't likely have gotten me anywhere. The more interesting point, I realized as I thought about it in a more relaxed setting, has to do with his insistence that if we believe something bad is a fulfillment of prophecy, then we should be passive in our acceptance of that state of affairs.

The fact is that people who rely on pessimistic Bible prophecy scenarios are often blatantly inconsistent on such things. Many of them believe, for example, that the Bible prophesies for the last days both the emergence of a large apostate church and a widespread spirit of moral anarchy. But here they do not simply sit back and accept these things as inevitable signs of the times. They preach against the World Council of Churches and denounce what they see as the errors of papalism. They also campaign against pornography and abortion-on-demand. Why do they do this if they also believe these phenomena are prophesied? Because they believe that obedience to the gospel requires us to speak out against evil, even if we have no realistic hope for success in stemming the tide, prior to God's final victory in history. If Jesus is to return during their lifetimes, they want to be found faithfully opposing all that dishonors his name, even if the things they oppose are prophesied in the Bible as signs that the end is in sight. But then why not also denounce unjust wars and oppressive racism and unbridled materialism? Shouldn't we want Jesus to find us taking our stand against such things, even if they too are signs that we are in the last days?

Two Cheers

I am not disappointed that dispensationalism—at least the kind that long held sway in the fundamentalist community—is on the decline as a widely used theological methodology. But I do want to be sure we give it a proper farewell. So before the older variety of dispensationalism becomes an almost invisible presence to mainstream evangelicals, I want to offer two cheers in celebration of its accomplishments.

My first cheer is directed toward its *spiritual* merits. By their fruits ye shall know them, and I want to repeat my testimony here that I have benefited greatly from the spiritual fruits of dispensationalism. Throughout my childhood and teenage years, the majority of my spiritual mentors were dispensationalists. When I first began my personal devotional life, it was a Scofield Study Bible I read on a daily basis. Dispensationalist charts hung on the walls at the Bible conference where I worked during my high school summers. At youth rallies and Bible clubs, from itinerant teachers and radio evangelists (including the founder of the seminary I now lead!), in handbooks and magazines—in all of these contexts I learned the dispensationalist way of "rightly dividing the Word of Truth."

It was in those same environs that I learned many other things. And they were precious things. Later on, when I heard my Reformed friends say negative things about what they saw as dispensationalism's heresies, the criticisms never rang very true to my ears. Dispensationalists were supposed to downplay the relevance of the Old Testament for the Christian life—yet some of the best preaching I've ever heard on the Psalms was from dispensationalists. Dispensationalist theology drew strict theoretical boundaries between Jesus as Israel's Messiah and Jesus as the Lord of the church; but the Jesus I learned about from dispensationalists was a heaven-sent Savior who showed a matchless love for both Gentile and Jew. The dispensationalist perspective was supposed to undercut Christian social concerns—but long before I had ever heard of Mother Teresa I saw dispensationalists lovingly embrace the homeless in inner-city rescue missions. Whatever the defects of the older dispensationalism as a theological perspective, it embodied a spirituality that produced some of the most Christlike human beings I have ever known.

The second cheer is for the *intellectual* content of dispensationalism. Undergirding the theological specifics of the dispensationalist system is a theory about how historical change occurs. The critics of dispensationalism have often gotten so bogged down with the theological details that they have not looked carefully at the strengths of this more basic pattern of thought.

The older dispensationalism placed a very strong emphasis on a highly conflictual understanding of historical change. History moves from crisis to crisis, with the major dispensations often being ushered in by cataclysmic events. In the "normal" historical flow, things do not tend to get better. Christian hope is based not in a trust about anything intrinsic to the historical process but in the firm expectation that in the end *God will intervene* from outside the process.

Think of what this meant to the dispensationalists of a hundred years ago. As they anticipated the beginning of a new century, they were not optimistic about the world situation. They expected wars and rumors of wars. They feared the coming of the antichrist. In contrast, think of the mood of mainline Protestantism at the time. Liberal theologians were expressing a deep faith in historical progress. They saw the kingdom of God expanding in its influence. The twentieth century was to be "the Christian Century." War and poverty and famine would soon be virtually eliminated from the face of the earth.

Now, I ask: who had a better sense of what was going to happen in the twentieth century? It seems obvious to me that Protestant liberalism was simply wrong in its predictions, whereas much of the dispensationalist scenario was vindicated. Why have we not given the dispensationalists more credit for their insights? Who was better equipped to prepare their children for the now much-heralded demise of Enlightenment optimism—the dispensationalists, or their cultured despisers?

The answers seem to point clearly in the direction of vindication for the dispensationalists' general view of history. To be sure, this does not mean we dare not criticize the details of their hermeneutical system or their "Bible prophecy" schemes. But in offering our criticisms we would do well to appreciate the theological impulses undergirding their efforts. It is because of these theological instincts, as well as their very real spiritual gifts, that I lift up two cheers for the older dispensationalists.

"Millennial Madness"

I said above that dispensationalism is not as popular these days as it used to be *as a theological methodology*. But this doesn't mean it is no longer popular as a way of looking at the future. Several years ago I heard a theologian complain that we evangelicals don't pay much attention anymore to the important biblical teaching that Jesus is coming again. He certainly can't complain about this now. As you read this, the year 2000 has arrived, and there has been widespread interest in the spiritual significance of this change of calendar. Novels that deal with the Rapture and the Second Coming are best-sellers right now. And the Israeli government is nervous about Christian groups who want to come to Israel to wait for the Messiah to return, fearing that they might stir up trouble in order to hasten "the sign of his coming." As I surf the cable channels on my television set, it is difficult to avoid snatches of "prophetic" teachings.

In the past year or two I have had several interviews with reporters who have wanted to talk about "millennial madness." I tell them I do believe in the Second Coming. For one of them I even quoted what our Fuller Seminary Statement of Faith has to say on the subject: "God's redemptive purpose will be consummated by the return of Christ to raise the dead, to judge all people according to the deeds done in the body, and to establish his glorious kingdom."

Jesus *is* coming again! The Christians who are so obsessed these days with "end times" matters are right on this point. But they are not right in their speculations about when and where he will appear. They don't pay close enough attention to what Jesus actually said to his apostles just before he ascended into heaven. So I've been telling the reporters to look up this verse in the Bible:

It is not for you to know the times or dates the Father has set by his own authority. But you will receive power when the Holy Spirit comes on you; and you will be my witnesses in Jerusalem, and in all Judea and Samaria, and to the ends of the earth.

ACTS 1:7–8

I tell the reporters that as a theological educator I am more interested in training people for "the ends of the earth" than for "the end times." I'll keep listening in on Bible prophecy discussions, and occasionally I will learn about some things I need to keep an eye on as I read my newspaper. But I also will take seriously the Lord's admonition that it is not for me to know "the times or dates." This I *can* know, however, and for this I will hold myself responsible as I think about how I am to live in a world full of tensions, maybe even the tensions that will lead to the last days: "You will receive power . . . and you will be my witnesses."

CHAPTER TEN

UNDERSTANDING SISTER HELEN'S TEARS

When my Catholic friends start reminiscing about the nuns who taught them in parochial schools, I maintain a respectful silence. I have never even set foot in a Catholic school. I do have some inkling, however, of what it is like to be taught by a nun. Miss O'Connell wasn't a nun during the time she was my seventh grade public school teacher, but she entered a convent at the end of our year together. I even have a sneaking suspicion I gave her a little nudge in that direction.

Most of the women who taught me during my four years in the Watervliet, New York, public school system were Irish Catholics: Miss O'Brien, Miss Byrne, and Miss Fogarty dominated my world in those days.

And, of course, the nun-to-be, Helen O'Connell. She was both very Irish and very Catholic, and if anyone had ever mentioned the separation of church and state to Miss O'Connell, I'm sure she would have thought the idea preposterous. To be sure, the Lord's Prayer, the Ten Commandments, and "God Bless America" were the standard fare of everyday public school piety in the early 1950s. But Miss O'Connell was not one to settle for generic civil religion.

She made the sign of the cross at our opening devotions, and her classroom conversations were liberally sprinkled with references to the Holy Father and the Blessed Virgin and—one of her favorite subjects—the Blarney Stone.

I flustered Miss O'Connell. For the most part her irritation with me had to do with a touch of the smart-aleck and know-it-all attitude I was wont to display rather frequently in those days. But Miss O'Connell's frustration also had to do more specifically with my propensity for issuing theological challenges to her reflexive Catholicism. "We Protestants don't believe in the pope," I would tell her in the middle of one of her brief classroom homilies. And then her neck would begin to redden, soon to be followed by a full-scale blush and then a nervous transition into another topic.

She made her announcement on the last day of regular classes in our seventh grade school year. "I have something to tell you, boys and girls"—the blush was already there, and we knew it was an important topic. "I am leaving this school. God has called me to be a nun. I will soon be entering the convent." She quickly turned to record some final piece of classroom business on the blackboard. But just before she did—just as she finished uttering the word "convent"—she glanced in my direction. Our eyes met very briefly. Hers were full of tears. Much to my surprise, I too felt like crying. Many hours later, alone in my bedroom, I did let the tears flow.

I have wondered many times since whether Miss O'Connell's tears that day had anything specifically to do with me. Was she worried about my soul? Had she come to think of me as one of her spiritual-pedagogical failures? Did our little religious tug-of-war have anything to do with her decision to take the habit? Could it even be that she felt, in the spiritual passion of my own classroom argumentativeness, a kindred spirit?

In my more rational moments it seems obvious I'm exaggerating the significance of that tearful glance. Surely my worries have more to do with my own memories of adolescent awkwardness than with the inner workings of Helen O'Connell's soul. But for all of that, the questions have nagged at me over the decades. And so one night a few years ago, when I was back in the Watervliet area on business, I began dialing from my motel room the numbers of O'Connells listed in the phone book, asking about a Helen O'Connell who had been my seventh grade teacher in a public school just before she had become a nun.

I connected on the fourth attempt. "I'm sure you're talking about a distant cousin of my husband's," the woman said. "I never really got to know Sister Helen," she said. "But I did meet her briefly once at a family gathering. Unfortunately, though, you're a little too late to contact her. I read in the paper a month or so ago that she died."

I had wanted to write Sister Helen a letter. I wanted to tell her I was sorry for my youthful arrogance. I wanted to tell her that I helped to get the Los Angeles Evangelical-Roman Catholic dialogue started, that I enjoy reading Henri Nouwen, and that sometimes I go to a Benedictine monastery to pray. I also wanted to tell her that even though I lacked the categories for saying so on the last day of seventh grade, I admired her decision to become a nun, that even then I knew deep in my heart she was doing so because she loved God very much.

It was too late to write that letter to Sister Helen. But a year later I found myself once again in the Watervliet area. After preaching at a church service in a nearby city on a Sunday morning, I drove to what had been Miss O'Connell's parish church. The late-morning mass at Saint Patrick's was still going on when I got there. I knelt with the rest of the worshipers for the prayers of the people.

When the congregation prayed for the souls of those who have died, I thanked the Lord for Helen O'Connell and for the mystery of those tears she shed on the day she told us she had been called to be a nun. I thanked God for Vatican II and for all of the good things that have been happening in Protestant-Catholic relationships since the last day of my seventh grade school year. And I asked the Lord to forgive the spiritual arrogance not only of a thirteen-year-old school boy but of an adult evangelical who has not yet lost all of the spiritual smart-aleckyness that lurked in that adolescent soul. And kneeling there in Helen O'Connell's church, I once again shed a few tears.

I still have some fairly strong disagreements with Roman Catholicism. And I am not yet prepared to dismiss all of those differences as minor misunderstandings. But I am glad for the brief exposure to Catholic pedagogy I had in the seventh grade. Sister Helen, rest in peace!

Evangelical Anti-Catholicism

During the past few years I have been part of a group of Roman Catholic and evangelical Protestant leaders—"Evangelicals and Catholics Together"—who have issued calls to new patterns of cooperation and understanding between our respective communities of faith. Our documents, whose drafters and signers include persons representing a variety of evangelical and Roman Catholic organizations, have placed a strong emphasis on the beliefs and concerns we hold in common. In contrast to much of mainline Protestantism and, to some degree, of Eastern Orthodoxy, Roman Catholics and evangelicals still have a strong commitment to evangelism and missionary activity. We believe much can be gained by working for more trust and cooperation.

Our documents have received considerable publicity. And they evoked some strong negative reactions, at least in the evangelical community. I have received widely circulated copies of letters and articles in which we evangelical endorsers of the document are accused of betraying the cause of the Protestant Reformation. Some of the correspondence we have received even crosses the boundary into the "hate mail" category. This situation points to the fact that the relationship between evangelicals and Roman Catholics is one that carries much historical and emotional baggage.

The baggage was certainly heavy when I was growing up. In good part, of course, the hostility toward Catholicism was spelled out in doctrinal terms. Catholics believed things we did not believe—things, furthermore, we thought *no one* should believe. In this sense, what we saw as the errors of Romanism were in a quite different order from the heresies of Protestant liberalism. We saw the liberals as believing *less* than we did, whereas the problem with Catholics was that they believed *more*. Liberals wanted to reduce the amount of "supernatural" beliefs associated with Christianity; but our evangelical arguments with Roman Catholics were never over that kind of reductionism. Indeed, if anything, we have found Catholics to be a little *too* inclined toward supernatural explanations. While, for example, we evangelicals have insisted in our arguments with liberals that it is important to believe in a literal virgin birth, Catholics upped the supernaturalist ante by telling us that we also need to accept the dogma of Mary's assumption, body and soul, into the heavenly regions. We evangelicals passionately argued that real water miraculously changed into real wine at Cana in Galilee, but we could sound like religious skeptics when we responded to the Catholic insistence that real wine regularly turns into the real blood of Christ in the Eucharistic celebration.

I think I was exposed to the worst of evangelical anti-Catholicism in my youth. I know that on occasion I heard "Bible prophecy" teachers proclaim with considerable self-confidence that the pope was the antichrist. I also had firsthand experience with evangelicals who believed that Catholics were in bondage to pagan beliefs, and that the only hope any Catholics had for salvation was that they would get to heaven "in spite of what their church teaches." These negative assessments had their influence on me, especially when they came from the mouths of evangelicals who had themselves been converted (including a number of ex-priests making the evangelical rounds in those days) from "Rome's pagan darkness."

But the impact of these verdicts was always held in tension for me with the friendships I had with flesh-and-blood Catholics. I had serious conversations with some of these friends about theological and spiritual matters, and they did not seem to fit the stereotypes being reinforced from evangelical pulpits. Indeed, they often struck me as genuine allies engaged in a common effort to resist the very obvious paganisms that tempted us in the adolescent culture of the day.

Some Good Company

I find myself in pretty good evangelical company as I assess my instinctive sense that it is a good thing for us to explore common ground with Roman Catholics. Take, for example, the great nineteenth-century "Old Princeton" theologian Charles Hodge. In his doctrinal disputes—and he was involved in many of them—he was a firm opponent of anything that departed from Calvinist orthodoxy. Yet he also insisted that "the cause of Protestantism suffers materially from undiscriminating denunciations heaped upon the church of Rome."[1] Hodge gave one of his essays the title "Is the Church of Rome part of the Visible Church?" and he answered his question with a strong affirmative. To be sure, he acknowledged, "the order and teaching of the Romish Church is in many respects corrupted and overlaid by false and soul-destroying abuses," but for all of that "the great body of people constituting the Roman Catholic Church do profess the essentials of the true Christian religion, whereby many of them bear the image of Christ, and are participants of His salvation."[2]

Or take the example of another nineteenth-century evangelical stalwart, Dwight L. Moody. In his biography of Moody, Wheaton College professor Lyle Dorsett quotes the text of a letter the evangelist received in 1875 from a Catholic monk in Wales. "I must send you one word of affectionate greetings in our Precious Redeemer's name," the monk wrote, "to say how rejoiced I am to hear and read of your powerful gifts from 'The Father of Lights,' 'good and perfect gifts' indeed." The monk went on to observe that while his community engaged in "the perpetual adoration of the Holy Sacrament," he and his fellow monks also preached "Jesus only as perfect, finished, and present salvation to all who are willing to receive Him. And the only work of the evangelist is to give knowledge of salvation to His people." Dorsett observes that Moody took encouragement from this letter; he then provides several other examples of the way in which Moody refused to conform to the anti-Catholicism that typified the evangelical movement of his day.[3]

I appreciate the wisdom of D. L. Moody and Charles Hodge on this subject. We evangelicals today, though, have even more to build on in extending hands of Christian fellowship to Roman Catholics. The Second Vatican Council, which in the 1960s opened the windows to the breezes of theological change in the Roman Catholic Church, is one of the great spiritual events of my lifetime. The key documents of Vatican II not only confirm the impression that important changes have taken place in Catholic life and thought, they also have some important positive theological lessons to teach the rest of the Christian world, including the evangelical world.

Not only has the theological distance between evangelicals and Catholics diminished in recent decades, but we have also been drawn closer together in matters of practical spirituality. In the early 1970s I accepted an assignment from an evangelical magazine to write a reflective report on a large conference of "Catholic charismatics" held in the fieldhouse at the University of Notre

Dame. It was an exciting event—much inspirational singing, good Bible teaching, many testimonies of Catholics who had come to realize the presence of the risen Christ in their lives through the power of the Holy Spirit. One experience stands out as a revelation to me of the new face of Roman Catholicism. During one of the evening services, as the crowd of thousands sang "His Name Is Wonderful," I saw an elderly nun, wearing the traditional habit, with hands upstretched to heaven and eyes closed, singing the words with such an expression of devotion that it seemed to me she must be looking directly into the face of the Savior.

Talking Past Each Other

In my own involvement in evangelical-Roman Catholic dialogue, I am struck by the impression that we often talk past each other in theological discussions. The most common pattern is one wherein evangelicals are thinking about salvation issues when Roman Catholics are thinking about the corporate life of the church.

This pattern expressed itself in a poignant manner at a meeting held at Fuller Seminary about the tensions between evangelicals and Catholics in the Latino community in southern California. A Mexican-American Pentecostal pastor told of his experience of attending a Catholic funeral mass for a young man who had been killed in a gang-related incident. "The boy who died was a close friend of a young man in my church, so I went to the funeral. Dozens of gang members were there," he said. "I thought to myself, 'What a wonderful opportunity to talk to these young people about what it means to give their lives to Jesus Christ!' But the whole funeral was just 'business as usual.' They just did a regular requiem mass. It was taken for granted that everyone was a Christian, and there was no real explanation of what the gospel was all about!" A Mexican-American priest immediately responded to this complaint: "'Business as usual' is exactly what we *want* them to experience. We want to expose them to *church*. We want them to experience what it is like to deal with the issues of life and death in the normal context of the community of the faithful. Let them have a taste of what the 'ordinary' church is all about!"

This is a fairly typical evangelical-Roman Catholic exchange. The evangelical wants questions about "how we are saved" to be addressed explicitly; he wants unbelievers to be invited to accept the message of salvation as it is set forth in simple and direct terms. The Roman Catholic wants to expose the unbelievers to the "normal" rituals of the church community in the hope that the exposure itself—quite apart from a conscious response to a gospel invitation—will be a means of grace.

After this initial exchange at the meeting, though, we worked toward a richer and more nuanced understanding on both sides. The Catholics admitted it might be good to issue a call to disciple-ship in the situation described; the evangelicals conceded that the Holy Spirit can work in a covert manner, drawing sinners to Jesus by the less-than-fully-explicit communal witness of the Christian community as it gathers to do its "business as usual."

Remaining Differences

Real differences do remain, nonetheless. We evangelicals do give higher priority to "salvation" questions and Roman Catholics to "corporate" ones. An obvious case in point is the issue of "pray-ing to the saints." Evangelicals criticize popular Catholic piety in this area by insisting that Jesus Christ alone is our mediator. Catholics respond with the insistence that prayers to the saints are an exercise in Christian community, that is to say, we talk about spiritual matters with our fellow Christians who are still on earth—why not also talk with those who have already gone to heaven?

Evangelicals worry that prayers to the saints will detract from Christ's redemptive work. Catholics answer these concerns by

pointing out that prayers to the saints are not salvifically significant, that they are merely an expanded version of churchly fellowship. Here again, part of the problem is that we are talking past
each other: Evangelicals do not want a relationship to a saint to
stand in the way of total reliance on Jesus; Catholics want us to
have a much richer experience of the community of the faithful.

But there *is* more to it than that. Even after we recognize
these differing theological dynamics, there are still important issues
to debate. We evangelicals worry about what happens to us when
we earthly Christians have too many "heavenly" friends. Don't these
saints take on an "exalted" status that can draw us away from our
supreme loyalty to Christ—even when we insist we are only having friendly conversations with them? And Catholics will respond
that the "just Jesus and me" patterns of evangelicalism do detract
from a rich understanding of the fullness of the church—that a
proper recognition of Christ's saving mission will acknowledge that
one of the important things Christ desires to accomplish in our
lives is that we be ushered into an expanded experience of the
Christian community.

These are, to be sure, meaningful issues we need to keep chal-
lenging each other to clarify further. There is no question in my
mind that at least some of the criticisms Catholics raise in discussions with us point to real defects in evangelical thought and practice. But I am not ready to concede *too* much in these discussions.
Catholicism has done a wonderful job of theological and spiritual
self-critique in the twentieth century. But the evangelical movement
has also experienced renewal—in a way that equips us to prod
Roman Catholics toward more renewal, even as we admit that we
need to continue to learn from our Catholic friends.

CHAPTER ELEVEN

"REAL" EVANGELISM

In my earlier discussion of Jewish-Christian relationships, I said that I see Jewish evangelism as a nonnegotiable obligation. Having committed myself to this very sensitive form of evangelism, it will come as no surprise that I also see evangelism as such—to the Gentile as well as to the Jew—as something about which we can make no compromises. But it is worth making the point anyway, because evangelism is not a high-priority item in many Christian circles these days. Some folks are offended by the very idea of any attempt to convert non-Christians. Others pay lip service to it but don't pursue it very aggressively. Still others support evangelism by redefining it in such a way that evangelism becomes simply "bearing witness"—in the sense that bearing witness, and therefore evangelism, takes place even when there is no felt need to *say* anything about the content of the gospel. So I want to make it clear I not only support the task of evangelism, but I also see it in terms of "real" evangelism. I see the evangelistic task in basically the same way as those who engaged in it when the smell of sawdust hung heavy in the air.

By *basically* I mean this: As I view the traditional evangelical understanding of evangelism, it contains these three components:

- Evangelism has to do with *conversion*—we want people's *lives* to be changed.
- It has to do with the *experience* of conversion—we want people to *know* they have been saved.
- It has to do with a conversion experience that includes the acceptance of some important *cognitive content*—we want people to understand and believe the *truth* of the gospel.

I contend that these three components are necessary in order for "real" evangelism to take place. They are the kinds of things one expects to find in any evangelical's understanding of what evangelism is really about.

So I want to take a closer look at the components, thinking about why some people—including many in the church—are scandalized by the very idea of the kind of evangelistic project that contains these features. I want to try to place the best possible interpretation on what the critics are concerned about, examining the ways in which the understanding of evangelism I have outlined—conversionist in its aim, experiential in its spirit, and cognitivist in its emphasis on the importance of a message—holds up under a critical inquiry that takes seriously the sense of scandal some people associate with the very idea of evangelism.

"In" versus "Out"

Some people are scandalized by the *polarized thinking*—the "us-versus-them" mentality—often associated with an enthusiasm for evangelism. The attempt to convert people is based on the assumption that some people are "in" and some are "out." Doesn't this promote an unhealthy polarization in the human community, and even in the church community?

This is an important concern, to be sure. And it deserves a candid response—so here it is: On one level it does seem impossible for Christians ultimately to avoid polarization. The biblical writers employ all kinds of pairs of polarizing terms: righteous and unrighteous, saved and lost, sheep and goats, weeds and wheat, church and world, faithful and unfaithful, and so on. The notion that some may ultimately be "in" and others "out" may be offensive, but it is an offense that, from a biblical perspective, seems necessary to work with.

But note that I keep throwing in the word *ultimately*. The division of humankind into two fundamental categories is a Judgment Day reality, and it is God who will do the dividing. We have no business rushing to judgment in this regard. A healthy involvement in evangelism does not require that we proceed with a clear confidence in our ability to know who is "in" and who is "out." Indeed, that kind of confidence is most accurately described as a spiritual arrogance. Nothing I have said by way of explaining my own commitment to a conversionist mode of evangelism is meant to encourage such an attitude.

Take, for example, my insistence on people becoming *aware* of their converted status. In saying that being aware of conversion is an important element in being converted, I do not mean to insist that you have to *know* you are in a positive saving relationship to Jesus Christ in order to *be* in a positive saving relationship to Jesus Christ. The distinction between what we know we are and what we actually are is an important one. A person can be pregnant without knowing she is pregnant. A person can be the heir to a significant fortune without being aware of it yet. And it is important to allow that much the same may hold true in the matter of personal redemption. The theological questions at stake in discussions of the redemptive status of people who have never heard the gospel proclaimed seem to me to be enormously weighty ones; they deserve to be treated with tentativeness and even with an appropriate sense of awe in the presence of divine mystery. We can let ourselves experience that kind of awe and still feel strongly that being "in" hasn't properly or fully happened until a person comes to some awareness of having participated personally in the benefits of Christ's atoning work. This way of stating the case permits some flexibility in understanding what *counts* as accepting God's gift of redemption in Jesus Christ, and it also allows for a saving faith that is not yet a well-formed faith.

I find this flexibility helpful in thinking, for example, about the topic of "nominal Christians," that is, those persons who are members of churches—by baptism and other rites of Christian initiation—but who would be hard-pressed to articulate any way in which they have appropriated the claims of the gospel in their personal lives. Many of us evangelicals who have been involved in extensive dialogue with Roman Catholics in recent years have tried to clarify this issue in our own minds. The charge that we have regularly attempted to "proselytize" Roman Catholics—for example, in Latin American communities—points to the ways in which we have often assumed that to evangelize Catholics requires that we treat nominal Roman Catholics as non-Christians. This presumption is not necessary to the evangelistic task. We can call Roman Catholics to a deepening of their faith by the personal appropriation of the claims of the gospel without assuming that in doing so we are calling them from spiritual death to spiritual life. The only assumption we need to defend in this regard is that it is a good thing for people who are not conscious of the benefits of the gospel in their own lives to become aware of the personal appropriation of those benefits.

Less Talk?

Some people are also scandalized by the *intellectualism* of the sawdust trail approach. When we insist, as I have, that evangelism, when it fulfills its proper aims, brings persons to assent to certain cognitive claims, doesn't this stance run the risk of intellectualizing Christian commitment?

There is an irony of sorts to be considered here. Fundamentalism is widely known for its anti-intellectualism—this is the pattern analyzed with such skill by Mark Noll in *The Scandal of the Evangelical Mind*. But a proper understanding of fundamentalism requires clarity about the *sense* in which it is anti-intellectual: Fundamentalists oppose the kind of thinking that goes on in the academy; they are not given to careful, nuanced formulations of issues that are basic to the human condition; they often deal in clichés and proof texts. In this sense we might say that fundamentalists are anti-intellectual in their disdain for the patterns of academic scholarship.

But there is also an important sense in which fundamentalism is *highly* intellectual, in view of the fact that fundamentalists make much of the need for intellectual assent to specific doctrinal propositions. They aren't happy until they know that their candidates for conversion really believe the fundamentals.

This kind of attitude is often taken to an extreme. The view of evangelism I have described certainly does not require people to assent to a set of "heavy" theological propositions. Nor does it follow from my insistence on evangelism needing to aim at the acceptance of cognitive content that evangelism simply manifests the articulation of the cognitive content of the good news. Evangelization must surely value more than the mere acceptance of doctrines. Conversion not only changes the ways we *think* but also the ways in which we *feel* and *do*. The apostle Peter makes this abundantly clear: He wants us to be careful to prepare our *minds* but also to abandon evil, worldly *desires* and to engage in holy *conduct* (see 1 Peter 1:13–15). Evangelism must pay attention to all of these dimensions of our lives.

Indeed it may well be that much evangelistic activity will actually emphasize, at least on occasion, the feeling and doing parts more than the thinking. It is one thing to insist, as evangelical Christians have always rightly done, that evangelism must include the verbal articulation of the claims of the gospel; it is another thing to foster, as evangelicals have also done all too frequently, an orally compulsive approach to evangelism.

My own sensitivities on this score were shaped by the reading, many years ago now, of a marvelous little sermon by theologian Paul Tillich, published in his book *The Shaking of the Foundations.* Tillich's message was based on Mark 8, where Peter confesses that Jesus is the Christ. Tillich observed that immediately after Peter makes his confession, the Gospel writer tells us that "Jesus warned them not to tell anyone about him" (Mark 8:30). In the context of this passage the reason seems to be obvious: Peter's formal articulation of a point of theology was orthodox enough, but he did not yet understand its implications—Peter was offended by the thought, for example, that the Son of Man would have to suffer and be put to death.

In exploring the implications of this incident, Paul Tillich asked a question that made a lasting impression on me: Could it be that if Jesus were to teach in our midst today he would charge us not to talk about him with our contemporaries? "Should we not," Tillich asked, "at least be silent, in order to preserve the mystery of the words, instead of destroying their meaning by our common talk?"[1]

The relationship of silence to evangelism is a neglected topic. Those of us who care deeply about the evangelistic ministry of the church make much of the need for faithful utterance. But perhaps we should also think about the need for faithful silence. To be sure, Christians can retreat into silence out of timidity or fear or embarrassment. Those silences are regrettable. But there will also be on occasion the silences we struggle mightily within ourselves to maintain—those times when we hold our tongues against the overwhelming impulse to speak, because we sense that the time is not yet ripe for utterance or that we are not yet equipped to do the uttering. These painful silences, strategic silences we maintain for the sake of faithfulness, can themselves be the means of serving the cause of the One whose messianic mission called for occasions when he could not speak, lest he violate the mystery of the message with which he had been entrusted.

Individuals and Structures

Many Christians also complain that we evangelicals focus too much on the conversion of *individual persons.* This notion of individualism is especially offensive to those Christian thinkers who have insisted that, in our attempts to transform human life in the light of the gospel, we must concentrate on changing social structures. They are deeply disturbed by evangelism programs that ignore the "systemic" and corporate dimensions of human life.

This is a topic that has greatly exercised me as well. My first book appeared in 1973, with the title *Political Evangelism.* In the opening paragraphs I assured my evangelical readers that I endorsed the popular evangelical slogan "Jesus saves." But, I went on to argue, it is important to be clear about what Jesus saves us *from* and what he saves us *for.* Jesus came to rescue us from the full ravages of sin that have pervaded the cosmos: spiritual sin, economic sin, political sin, familial sin, and so on. And he saves us for the new and abundant life we were designed for in accordance with God's creating and liberating purposes.

Evangelism, then, is the proclamation of a message that speaks words of healing and hope to the full scope of human brokenness. Fundamentalists were fond of singing that "Jesus paid it all." But they regularly failed to address the ways in which Christ's atoning work was a divine response to the structural issues of human interaction—the ways, for example, in which he paid the debt of our racism and sexism and consumerism as well as the more personal kinds of sins we pietists like to emphasize.

Indeed, the more I've thought about these issues the greater difficulty I've had in drawing clear lines between the personal and the structural. I actually learned many of my earliest lessons about God's deep concern about poverty and oppression during regular visits to fundamentalist skid-row rescue missions during my childhood. There, long before I knew anything about a "social gospel," I saw dedicated Christians offering a loving embrace to the addicted, the hungry, and the homeless. These fundamentalists knew that to evangelize a drunk meant asking him to let go of his enslavement to alcoholism. Why was this called "personal evangelism," in contrast, say, to the so-called "structural" or "social" approach of those who believe that to accept Jesus properly also means to let go of deeply ingrained gender biases and racial prejudices? Fully to accept the good news about Jesus Christ is to be willing to give up, in a very personal way, *all* of those things—habits, attitudes, assumptions, and convictions, whether they have to do with sex or the marketplace or political ideologies—that keep us as individuals from full submission to Christ's lordship.

Nor can we separate these concerns from our evangelistic approach to those individuals who are the special victims of social, political, and economic oppression. Can we preach good news to political prisoners and exploited peasants without speaking to the conditions of their structural helplessness? Were the black slaves of North America simply wrong when they failed to distinguish clearly between the freedom offered by the gospel and liberation from the yoke of plantation slavery?

Changing Hearts, Changing Societies

Back in the days of South African apartheid, I often illustrated the importance of addressing the structural dimensions of human life by imagining a miraculous result from a single effort at mass evangelism. Suppose Billy Graham were to hold a crusade in South Africa, and every single person in the country, whether by being physically present at the meeting or by watching on television, were to make a personal commitment to Jesus Christ as Savior and Lord. Would this cure South Africa of its racism? No. The next morning all the apartheid apparatus would still exist. Laws would have to be rewritten. Prejudices would have to be unlearned. The educational system would have to be reformed. The evangelical slogan "changed hearts will change society" is clearly inadequate in such a situation. To be sure, the *motivation* to bring about change can result from millions of individual wills being redirected toward the love and service of a divine Savior. But individual conversions do not automatically bring about structural change.

In one sense, evangelicals have always known this. We have simply been highly selective in applying our insights. I once argued with a man who insisted that civil rights legislation was misguided. He professed a deep concern about racial attitudes, but he was convinced the only way to change racists was "to win them, one by one." On another occasion, however, I heard this same man holding forth about the evils of teaching evolutionism in the public schools. "We need to go to our school boards and complain about this," he was telling some Christian friends. "Our schools need to be reclaimed, and we have to do it by getting to the people who can change the policies!" I saw my opening. "I'm not convinced of that as the right approach," I said, breaking into the conversation. "Evolutionism is a matter of individual prejudice, and I think the only effective approach is to win the evolutionists, one by one!" He got my point—although later I did have to explain to the others that I hadn't really meant what I said.

Softly and Tenderly

In those areas where evangelicals do take the "big" structural issues seriously, they often manifest a crusading spirit. This is not a laudable trait. When I see this pattern emerging, I often wish for an infusion of some of the gentler features of the sawdust trail.

A few decades ago, historian Sandra Sizer wrote a fascinating book about nineteenth-century evangelical hymns titled *Gospel Hymns and Social Religion.*[2] She identified two strands of evangelistic imagery in the hymns she studied. The first are the images associated with what she calls "imperial mission," as found, for example, in this familiar missionary hymn:

> *From Greenland's icy mountains, from India's coral strand,*
> *Where Afric's sunny fountains roll down their golden sand;*
> *From many an ancient river, from many a palmy plain,*
> *They call us to deliver their land from error's chain.*

In these lines the language clearly emphasizes the need to conquer new territory so as to deliver the inhabitants from their confused lives. This imagery stands in contrast to the gentler songs Sandra Sizer identified with the "rescue mission" motif, as in this hymn:

> *Let the lower lights be burning!*
> *Send a gleam across the wave!*
> *Some poor fainting, struggling seaman*
> *You may rescue, you may save.*

I prefer this latter motif. It expresses the kind of evangelical spirit that issues gentle calls to hurting people to join us in a place of safety—in contrast to the militant pronouncements of would-be conquerors of new territories.

Nor am I troubled by the individual focus of the "softly and tenderly" approach. One way in which critics of evangelical "soul-winning" efforts frequently make their case is by complaining about our "me and Jesus" understanding of the Christian life. I don't find this kind of criticism very convincing. I care about structural issues, to be sure—but when I focus on the basics I still want to empha-size the need for individual people to get right with God. And the only way for this to happen is to enter into a "me and Jesus rela-tionship." Certainly I would never claim that this is all there is to the Christian life. Far from it! But a personal relationship with Jesus Christ is the foundation on which everything else rests. Sin does afflict our lives on all levels—our interpersonal relations, our political lives, our family patterns, our economic transactions; but sin also has its beginning in the rebellion of individual hearts. Help-ing individual people find their way Home is a crucial task. We can't have "real" evangelism without it.

CHAPTER TWELVE

"PREACHING THE BLOOD"

As I was growing up, I frequently heard my father and his evangelical clergy friends grade their colleagues on their theological orientation. Someone would ask: "The new guy at First Baptist—where does he stand?" The answer: "Well, I haven't really talked with him much myself, but Joe knows a couple who goes to that church and they say he's pretty sound."

Soundness was the standard benchmark for making these evaluations. "Pretty sound" was pretty good; it meant that when push came to shove you could expect this person to stand up for what we all knew were "the fundamentals"—Virgin Birth, Bodily Resurrection, Second Coming, and the like. "Very sound" was even better. This meant the person was even willing to *initiate* some of the pushing and shoving when necessary.

There was one piece of evaluation, however, that was reserved for special manifestations of evangelical orthodoxy: "He preaches the blood." This was a high compliment. People who preached the blood wanted to be like the apostle Paul, who desired nothing more than to "preach Christ crucified" (1 Corinthians 1:23). And, like Paul, they were willing to live with the disdain of their more "sophisticated" ministerial colleagues—because they knew this was a message seen as "a stumbling block to Jews and foolishness to Gentiles, but to those whom God has called, both Jews and Greeks, [as] Christ the power of God and the wisdom of God. For the foolishness of God is wiser than man's wisdom, and the weakness of God is stronger than man's strength" (1 Corinthians 1:23-25).

The Social Psychology

It is not difficult to apply some social psychology to this kind of emphasis. My father and his minister friends felt marginalized. Some of them, like my father, had studied at liberal seminaries where their evangelical witness was met with condescension on the part of faculty and students—a pattern perpetuated for those who went on to serve in mainline denominations. For example, one friend of our family regularly told horror stories of how he, a Presbyterian minister, was treated with disdain in his local presbytery because his congregation pledged minimal support to denominational mission programs, choosing instead to give generously to evangelical "faith missions." It is hardly surprising that such scorned folks would band together with others who saw themselves as a cognitive minority, taking common delight in their shared theological "foolishness."

Liberals would accuse these folks of adhering to "a slaughterhouse religion" in which a primitive deity could get over his anger only if he smelled the blood of his enemies—or of a fitting sacrificial substitute. But this critique only confirmed the evangelicals in their conviction that they were on the right side of the theological fence. Preaching the blood was a badge of honor.

These social dynamics are an important part of the picture. The evangelicals whose theological battles were the context for my early spiritual and theological formation insisted on a certain vocabulary in which the "power in the blood" and "being fools for Christ's sake" were prominent motifs. A willingness to use the right vocabulary was the criterion by which we separated who was "in" from who was "out." Cognitive minorities cannot survive without such tests of "soundness."

All of this must be recognized in order to understand what was going on when these folks insisted on preaching the blood. But this must also be said: They were right about a lot of these things. I am even convinced that in important ways their theological convictions have been vindicated by more recent developments. Indeed, my own sense is that they went wrong not by putting too strong an emphasis on the sacrifice offered up by the Savior on Calvary, but on those occasions when they stopped short of proclaiming the *full* "power in the blood."

The Post-Enlightenment Shift

We hear a lot these days about living in a "postmodern culture" in which there is widespread disillusionment with "Enlightenment thought." I'm a bit skeptical about the more extravagant claims being made about this alleged cultural shift. But it does seem safe to say at least this: Some of the ideas and emphases associated with the past movement (actually a collection of movements) referred to as the Enlightenment are not as popular as they used to be.

Enlightenment thinkers made much of the power of "the light of Reason" to illuminate the basic issues of life. Many of them were uncompromising in their insistence that the enlightened human mind was the highest standard of truth and meaning and value in the universe. And typically the scientific method was touted as the only reliable guide to finding the truth about reality. When this faith in science was wedded to what is referred to these days as "the myth of Progress," people were very optimistic about what scientific exploration could produce. Toward the end of the nineteenth century, for example, many people were proclaiming the birth of a new era of discovery. Humankind was on the threshold, they said, of solving many age-old problems—war, poverty, tribalisms, prejudice—by following the scientific path to Truth.

For many people this confidence was completely shattered by the events of the twentieth century. Two world wars—to say nothing of the unspeakable inhumanity of the Holocaust—made it difficult to believe we human beings were destined to use scientific knowledge to create new patterns of harmonious coexistence. Poverty, prejudice, ethnic hostility, polluted environments—all of these have proven to be quite resistant to whatever gains we might want to attribute to "Progress."

Thus the claims we hear these days about our "post-Enlightenment" cultural mood. To be sure, one can still find clear signs of a lingering fondness for Enlightenment thinking in the intellectual community. Not everyone has given up on "rational" solutions to the basic problems of the human condition. But we're also very aware of widespread reactions against the Enlightenment. Sociologist Peter Berger once observed that it would be wrong simply to see the members of the Church of Satan as rebelling against traditional Christianity—rather, they are thumbing their noses at their former university professors who taught them to put their trust in scientific rationality. And that is very likely also the best way to interpret contemporary culture's intense interest in occult practices and mystical religion. Not a few of the professors who taught their students about the glories of scientific progress have themselves joined witches' covens and neopagan cults in recent years!

In today's cultural environment, to label the "blood sacrifice" theology of my father and his clergy colleagues as "primitive" would not automatically be an insult. Primitive is "in" these days, you see. Postmodern people are fascinated by premodern worldviews. And the current disillusionment with Enlightenment thought has also had its positive effects within the Christian community. The older liberalism—the kind my father and his friends saw as the major threat to evangelical orthodoxy—has lost some of its appeal. Not that it has disappeared altogether—far from it. But in those mainstream Protestant circles where blood sacrifice themes would have been summarily dismissed in the past, there is a new interest in more traditional—even Catholic and Orthodox—understandings of the Eucharist.

Three Historical Arguments

I once accepted an invitation to be part of a panel discussion at a secular university campus, reflecting on the topic "The Past, Present, and Future of Religion in America." I was one of four invited speakers. The others were a rabbi, a Roman Catholic priest, and a mainline Protestant theologian. The program lasted for a entire day and consisted of four sessions. In the first, we each talked about the past involvement of our religious communities in American culture, then our present involvement, and finally our thoughts about our future involvement. In the evening we talked with each other and answered questions from the audience.

That evening the first question from a person in the audience was addressed to me. It went like this: "Dr. Mouw, I think I understand better now, from what you have explained, what an evangelical is. But it would be helpful to me if you could push it further by answering this question: What is it that you believe that the other three people on the panel do *not* believe?"

I immediately yielded to my ever-present impulse to quote a hymn. The Sunday before in our congregation we had sung "It Is Well with My Soul," and the third stanza had been running through my mind for several days. I quoted it to the university audience:

My sin—O the bliss of this glorious thought—
My sin, not in part, but the whole,
Is nailed to the cross, and I bear it no more;
Praise the Lord, praise the Lord, O my soul!
It is well with my soul, it is well, it is well with my soul.

This, I said, is a uniquely evangelical expression of faith.
The rabbi certainly is not going to sing about his sins being
nailed to the cross of Jesus Christ. And the priest, if he stands
for the kind of Catholicism Martin Luther preached against, is
not going to proclaim that because of the once-for-all sacrifice
on the cross he can proclaim it is forevermore well with his soul.
And much of mainline Protestantism has long been influenced
by a modernizing tendency that rejects "payment" and "sacrifice"
motifs in talking about the ministry of Jesus. (I should report
that as we left the stage that evening, the Roman Catholic pan-
elist told me I was right about sixteenth-century Catholicism,
but that he could with full confidence sing those words. Thank
the Lord for Vatican II!)

My fellow panelists represented the three historical arguments that are more than distant memories in the evangelical
heart and mind. The first argument was with the Jewish community, as the early church proclaimed that the sacrifices of temple Judaism were no longer necessary because Jesus had, as both
the Lamb who was slain and the great High Priest, fully satisfied God's demand that an adequate payment for sin be made.
The second argument took place in the sixteenth century, when
the Protestant Reformers proclaimed the "once for all"-ness of
the work of Christ in their criticisms of the Roman mass and
the selling of indulgences. And in response to the teachings of
liberal Protestants, evangelicals have defended the understanding of atonement associated with the biblical themes of payment,
sacrifice, and ransom.

All Is Not Well

All of this is good and important. "Preaching the blood" is at the center of my own understanding of the call to discipleship. Unfortunately, though, we have not always followed through on the far-reaching—I would even say the cosmic—implications of our understanding of the atoning work of Jesus Christ.

It is wonderful to be able to say "It is well with my soul." But the truth is that there is much else in the universe that is *not* "well." It is not well in abusive family systems. It is not well in ghettos and barrios. It is not well in African tribal villages or in Russian cities. All is not well in Seoul or Capetown or Buenos Aires or in the Balkan states. All is not well in Amsterdam or London or Beverly Hills.

The same God who looks upon my soul and declares my fundamental condition to be "well" for all eternity looks down on oppressive structures and impoverished cities and war-torn villages and grieves over the fact that all is not well in his creation. Someday all will be well—when Jesus declares that all things have been made new. But that day is not yet here. And so all who know that it is well with their souls must actively work toward the day when all will be well again in God's larger creation. And this enterprise we evangelicals have often failed to pursue with any sustained sense of urgency.

Personal And Cosmic

But this call to action must not detract from the power of the evangelical insistence on a *personal appropriation* of the atoning work of Christ, as expressed in Charles Wesley's thoroughly evangelical words:

> *And can it be that I should gain*
> *An int'rest in the Savior's blood?*

Died He for me, who caused His pain?
For me, who Him to death pursued?
Amazing love! How can it be
That Thou, my God, shouldst die for me?

But neither should we be insensitive to the cosmic implications of the Atonement, as set forth in that equally evangelical hymn written by Isaac Watts:

No more let sins and sorrows grow,
Nor thorns infest the ground;
He comes to make His blessings flow
Far as the curse is found,
Far as the curse is found,
Far as, far as the curse is found.

Both hymns are crucial to the message of a community that preaches the blood.

CHAPTER THIRTEEN

A WORD HIDDEN IN THE HEART

A nnie Dillard again, this time about the Bible verses she learned as a child:

> I had miles of Bible in memory: some perforce, but most by hap, like the words to songs. There was no corner of my brain where you could not find, among the files of clothing labels and heaps of rocks and minerals, among the swarms of protozoans and shelves of novels, whole tapes and snarls and reels of Bible.[1]

My brain too was filled as a child with "miles of Bible in memory." We had Bible memory contests in which we were rewarded for learning lists of verses—one from the Psalms, another from Genesis, another from Ephesians, another from Joshua, and so on. The same verses tended to show up at an important devotional ritual at our family dinner table: We owned a box of little colored cards with Bible verses printed on them—I think we bought it at a summer Bible conference—and after our nightly meal each family member would take a card and read it aloud. And then there was my favorite activity: "sword drills," where a verse would be shouted out to a roomful of kids with Bibles drawn, and the first one to find the verse would stand up and read it.

I've heard evangelical friends say they've had to work hard at "unlearning" the fundamentalist way of reading the Bible. I'm sure they are referring to the way a certain kind of *doctrine* of biblical authority shaped their early understanding. But for me this specific doctrine of biblical authority is not the primary fundamentalist legacy. What I was taught by fundamentalists was to permeate my consciousness with "Bible knowledge." And that is something I have never wanted to unlearn.

To be sure, these practices tended to promote a scattershot approach to appropriating the biblical message. We certainly were not encouraged to think about the *context* of the snippets we learned. And so we probably misunderstood the intended meanings of some of the verses that came to be lodged in our brains. But this really doesn't trouble me. The theological defects are miniscule when weighed against the benefits. "Thy word have I hid in mine heart" (Psalm 119:11 King James Version)—even if the contents worked their way into my brain in many little bits and pieces.

Much of this approach is lost today, and we cannot recover it. For one thing, a significant goal of these practices has been lost, namely, the learning of a common Christian mode of discourse. One big factor in causing us to lose sight of this goal has been the proliferation of Bible translations in recent decades. The snippets that filled my brain, as well as the brains of most of my fundamentalist contemporaries, were King James snippets. To be sure, this also meant that we misunderstood some of the texts we learned—I regularly have to correct the translation of a King James wording lodged in my brain. But here too the defects are outweighed by the benefits. The King James Bible gave us some good poetry along with our theology. Annie Dillard celebrates this feature of King James

English: "I wrote poems in deliberate imitation of its sounds, those repeated feminine endings followed by thumps, or those long hard beats followed by softness. Selah."[2]

Battling for the Bible

One of the periodicals that came into our home during my teenage years was *The Sword of the Lord*, edited by the Southern evangelist John R. Rice. Its style was, to put it mildly, confrontational and abrasive—later I learned that some evangelicals gave it the nickname "The Knife of the Spirit." Editor Rice regularly attacked Billy Graham for compromising with liberals, and he was hostile toward the larger "neo-evangelical" movement for what he perceived to be its apostate tendencies.

A one-frame *Sword of the Lord* cartoon stands out in my memory. It was a courtroom scene. The judge, sitting on a high bench, is labeled "The Word of God." Several men are lined up to take the witness stand: I know one was "Liberal" and another was "Neo-evangelical"; I think "Roman Catholic" and "Neo-orthodox" were also in the lineup. Another man, probably a clerk, was addressing the bench. His words: "But, your Honor, these men want to put *you* on trial!"

This was the concern that surfaced in the later "battle for the Bible," a major evangelical controversy stirred up by Harold Lindsell's 1976 book by that name. Lindsell and others insisted that to be an evangelical one must adhere to "strict inerrancy." This meant, among other things, that evangelicals were required to go to great lengths to "harmonize" the four Gospels into a smooth-flowing narrative. The most notorious example of how Lindsell himself applied this method was his argument that the different accounts of Peter's denial of Jesus (see Matthew 26:69–75; Mark 14:66–72; Luke 22:55–62; John 18:16–18, 25–27) had to be reconciled by asserting that the disciple actually issued six denials. Any evangelical who rejected this kind of approach, the strict inerrantists argued, was no better than those "biblical critics" who openly called into question the authority of God's Word.

Prominent in the arsenal of the battlers for the Bible has been the "slippery slope" argument, namely, that employing critical methods of biblical study will inevitably weaken our commitment to key evangelical teachings and emphases. I see no evidence that this prediction was a sound one. For example, *inerrant* is not a term of choice for most of my Fuller colleagues; we much prefer *infallible*. But we would never tolerate anyone in our midst saying that something the Bible clearly teaches is simply erroneous. Our theological discussions take it for granted that our views about the key issues of life must be brought into conformity to the teachings of the Scriptures.

The debate over inerrancy functioned as a "political" skirmish within the evangelical movement. It was an attempt to draw the boundaries that mark out evangelical identity in a restrictive manner. The arguments were more about methods of studying the Scriptures than they were about whether we have a right to reject something clearly taught by the biblical writers. The underlying question was whether we evangelicals are open to new ways of *discerning what the Bible teaches.*

As A. W. Tozer was fond of putting it, we can use all kinds of tools and methods for getting at the meaning of the Scriptures, but once the meaning is discovered, that specific meaning judges *us*—we never judge it. When the use of new critical tools is harnessed to a deep devotion to the Bible as an utterly reliable word from God, the results can greatly enrich our understanding of God's will for our lives.

The "Size" of Authority

My own irritation with the way strict inerrants make their case has to do with some personal history. Back in the days when

a few of us were urging evangelicals to be more involved in addressing social concerns, we regularly ran into resistance from people
who had an "inerrant" Bible that turned out nonetheless to be
rather limited in its scope of authority. We would try to convince
these folks that God cares deeply about the poor by quoting the Old
Testament prophets. In arguing with us, they did not deny that
Amos makes a powerful case for identifying with the oppressed.
Rather, they appealed to a dispensationalist framework by insisting that Amos was addressing a "theocracy" in a previous dispen-
sation, and that his views are not relevant for the Gentile church.
Their "inerrant" Bible, it turned out, contained a lot of material that
was, for them, little more than ancient history.

These experiences convinced me that there are deeper issues
about biblical authority than the defenders of inerrancy were
acknowledging. How "big" is our Bible? How do we understand "the
whole counsel of God" in a way that allows us to draw on the full
scope of God's revelation to humankind?

A more general concern about scope can be expressed by
thinking about literary categories rather than social concerns. By
focusing exclusively on the propositional character of revelation,
the strict inerrantists fail to account for the many other ways in
which the Bible provides us with utterly reliable guidance for our
lives. The Bible is more than a set of propositions requiring our
cognitive assent. It gives us prayers, dreams, visions, commands,
songs, complaints, pleadings, parables, love letters, and more—yet
inerrant isn't really the right word for explaining how these elements of the biblical record are an important part of the Bible's
authority. To be sure, the Bible is not *less* than a propositional message from the living God, a message that contains *truths* we must
believe and hold on to for our very lives. How we respond to what
the Bible tells us about God's dealings with humankind is a matter of eternal significance. But the Bible does also "tell" us important things in ways that cannot be reduced to simple propositions.

Words of Beauty

Shortly after I was named president of Fuller Seminary, I received a letter from a well-known evangelist, asking me about my family pedigree. Seeing the announcement about me in *Christianity Today,* he wondered whether I was related to Tunis Mouw, a fundamentalist pastor he had known. Was I his son? If so, did I intend to lead Fuller "back to the truth of God's Word"?

I wrote back. The preacher in question was my late uncle, a person whom I greatly admired, I told him. And, like my uncle, I am firmly committed to the truth of God's Word. I assured him that I want Fuller Seminary to be faithful to this truth. And I believe it *is* faithful—strongly so. At Fuller we believe that Jesus Christ came into the world to save sinners, and that proclaiming this message is of the utmost importance. Those convictions are not things we have to "go back to." We are still there.

I also told this evangelist that as a teenager I had attended youth rallies he had sponsored. I expressed my deep gratitude for his long-standing commitment to bringing the simple truths of the gospel to people like me. I owed him much, and I told him so. Then, in my letter, I quoted the first verse of the gospel song that served as the theme song of his ministry:

> Sing them over again to me,
> Wonderful words of life;
> Let me more of their beauty see,
> Wonderful words of life.
> Words of life and beauty,
> Teach me faith and duty:
> Beautiful words, wonderful words,
> Wonderful words of life.

At Fuller Seminary, I said, I have come to have an even deeper appreciation for the riches of the Scriptures, especially for what it means to ask the Lord to "let me more of their beauty see." Each year at Fuller we have students from at least sixty nations; they belong to 120 different denominations. We are educating both men and women for leadership in the kingdom. And, in the midst all of this diversity, there is a warm love for the Lord Jesus, a profound desire to learn more about his Word, and a passionate commitment to demonstrating that the gospel can transform human lives. In this context, the Lord is constantly teaching me new things about the riches of those "words of life" I heard about at the youth rallies this evangelist sponsored. I thanked him for teaching me to ask God to give me new lessons about the beauty of the Word, and I invited him to visit Fuller to see these things for himself. He never responded. But he is now learning his own lessons about the beauty of Jesus and his Word, directly in the Savior's presence.

Evangelicalism is blessed these days with new opportunities to understand the profound words of life given to us in the Scriptures. For some of us, these new lessons are expanded versions of what we first learned by submitting to the spiritual disciplines of Bible memory contests and "sword drills."

CHAPTER FOURTEEN

TOWARD A NEW WORLDLINESS

In 1656 John Reeve, the self-styled prophet of the British religious sect known as the Muggletonians, ridiculed the popular notion of a literal millennial kingdom. Reeve insisted that it is highly unlikely Jesus would want to return to earth to establish a one-thousand-year reign. After all, he observed, Jesus has "suffered here already" during the last time he lived on earth. Why would he want to come back as a politician and suffer again? Isn't one round of intense divine misery enough?

I must admit I'm sometimes tempted to add yet another consideration to Reeve's line of argument: Even if Jesus did *not* suffer enough during his first earthly tour of duty, I ask myself, isn't it likely he has by now had his fill of "Christian politics"? Hasn't at least his capacity for *political* suffering finally reached its limit? And can it be that it is the highly visible activity of "the Christian Right" during the past few decades that has pushed him over the edge?

In my more reflective moments I know better than to take these questions seriously. Jesus is long-suffering with our awkward attempts to be faithful to his will—and this applies to evangelical

143

activism as well. Nor do I really think that what has happened in recent decades has been a complete waste of time.

Past Withdrawal Patterns

I reentered the evangelical community after my years of graduate study with a passion for evangelical activism. The kind of evangelicalism in which I was raised had little interest in taking an active role in the public square. We saw ourselves as a remnant people in a world bound to get worse before the return of Christ. We saw our main task as, in the image Dwight L. Moody made popular, helping drowning people get into the lifeboats.

The titles of some of my early books tell the story of my sense of mission in promoting a change of perspective. As I have already told the story, *Political Evangelism* (1973) was a call for evangelicals to see political action, which they had long sedately shunned, as intimately linked to evangelism, which they had long passionately pursued. *Politics and the Biblical Drama* (1976) made a more sustained case for the centrality of political concerns in the biblical message. My 1980 book *Called to Holy Worldliness* directly addressed the question of how involvement in "the world" might be a way of pleasing God.

"Worldliness" had for a long time been a sort of naughty word among evangelicals. And not without some good reason. After all, the biblical writers can be quite negative about "the world"—an obvious case in point being the warning in John's First Epistle that we must not "love the world or anything in the world" (1 John 2:15). But a comprehensive theology of "the world" also has to take John 3:17 into account: "For God did not send his Son into the world to condemn the world, but to save the world through him." And needless to say, it has taken some effort for evangelical pietists to ignore this latter text, given its immediate proximity to what is surely the most quoted biblical verse among evangelicals—John 3:16.

Obviously these Johannine references contain two different senses of "the world." In the negative sense, to love the world is to conform to the patterns of evil that are presently so prominent in our fallen creation. In the positive sense, God nonetheless loves this world, the cosmos, which is presently distorted by those evil patterns that have resulted from the curse of sin; indeed God loves it so much that Jesus was sent to initiate a program of cosmic renewal. Thus the case for "holy worldliness."

A New Activism

During the heyday of the Moral Majority one of my former students wrote to tell me he had recently reread *Political Evangelism.* "In going back through this book," he said, "I was surprised to realize how the Moral Majority types could now read it and tell you they are doing exactly what you asked them to be doing back in the older days of 'otherworldliness.' Doesn't that bother you?" My answer was: Well, yes and no. The agenda of the Moral Majority—and of the more recent manifestations of the Christian Right—is not exactly what I had in mind when I wrote about the need for Christian activism. But neither do I see it as completely misguided.

Very little serious attention has been paid to the factors that have given rise to the wave of recent social activism among evangelicals. I think a key factor has been the sense of cultural desperation many of us have felt as secularism took on a new agenda in the "sexual revolution" of recent decades. In the past, we could observe the events of the larger society with some sense of detachment. But as pornography, homosexual rights, abortion-on-demand, rising divorce rates, sex education in the schools, and the like became increasingly prominent on the cultural agenda, evangelicals found it difficult to think of themselves as a remnant group capable of protecting itself from larger cultural movements and developments; the very fabric of family life was now threatened by these new trends.

This new sense of a cultural crisis threatening the very fabric of evangelical identity was also accompanied by a class shift among evangelicals. And so, sensing they now actually had some leverage to facilitate change, evangelicals entered the public square. Critics have often complained that the Christian Right has an almost myopic fixation on sexual and family issues. But for the new evangelical activists, this is hardly a legitimate criticism. Sexual and family issues are in fact at the heart of the cultural crisis that has inspired the new mood of activism.

The Need for Theology

The problem is, however, that the social-political arena is one area of life where evangelicals seem to be inclined toward dealing with complex issues by relying on slogans and proof texts. This was certainly the case when some of us first began urging a more active public involvement several decades ago. It was very clear in those days that evangelicalism—for all its professed interest in theological orthodoxy—had paid very little attention to questions about corporate life. My own informal survey, conducted by listening carefully to evangelical objections to my arguments in favor of social activism, showed that most evangelicals were operating with a small stock of proof texts in their address to this subject. Here are the four most frequently quoted to me:

- Matthew 26:11—"The poor you will always have with you," which many evangelicals apparently took as a word of encouragement to see to it that there were plenty of poor people around.
- Matthew 22:21—"Give to Caesar what is Caesar's, and to God what is God's"—as if God had simply given over to Caesar a

major portion of reality with no strings attached.

- Romans 13:1—"The authorities that exist have been established by God," which was taken as an unnuanced endorsement of the political status quo.
- John 18:36—Jesus' remark to Pilate that "my kingdom is not of this world."

The superficiality of using these verses in support of social inactivism can be seen by thinking about the larger context of this last Scripture text, namely, Jesus' comment to Pilate. No matter how we interpret this retort to Pilate's line of questioning, we should keep in mind the fact that Pilate's authority and Jesus' authority soon came into direct and unambiguous conflict. Have you ever thought about the fact, I have asked my evangelical audiences many times, that the resurrection was illegal? Pilate employed two legal strategies to keep Jesus' body in the tomb: First, he placed his seal on the stone that blocked the entrance—to break this seal was an illegal act; second, he assigned a military guard to stand watch at the tomb—to defy their presence was also to break the law. When Jesus burst forth from the tomb on Easter morning, then, he violated Pilate's authority twice over, breaking his seal and rendering the military guard powerless. The resurrection of Jesus Christ was the first act of Christian civil disobedience! Whatever Jesus meant when he told Pilate that his kingdom was not of this world, he did not mean to be granting Pilate the authority to cancel the resurrection or to stand in the way of anything else God is doing to transform the reality of his kingdom.

Evangelicals have in recent years developed a healthy sense of the need to think critically about the status quo. Undeniably, this is an advance. To be sure, we have not always acted in appropriate ways in terms of working out the practical implications of our social critique. But at least these days we no longer have to mount lengthy arguments designed to get evangelicals to recognize the need for active citizenship.

Cultivating Virtues

I would maintain that we evangelicals should not back off from our recent activism. But it is time to reflect further on the kind of people we ought to try to be as we pursue involvement in the world. Two virtues seem especially appropriate to cultivate in this regard: *patience* and *humility.*

For the patience part of the program, we may need to recover some of the spirit associated with the notion that we are a remnant people—and then to find those patterns of involvement that are appropriate to our remnant identity. We evangelicals seem to have a tendency to reduce our strategies to two basic options. Either we withdraw from public involvement, or we try to take over the public square. To do so rules out an important alternative: to stay in the public square without trying to take it over, working to promote righteousness with the clear understanding that we are sharing in God's own demonstration of patience with his rebellious creation.

Not that it is easy to hold all of this together. To be patient, for example, does not mean simply to stop worrying about patterns of life that are clearly in violation of God's revealed standards of righteousness. But proper patience does rule out public behaviors that stem from a spirit of self-righteousness. The antithesis between godliness and ungodliness is very real; yet it is discernible not only in the larger patterns of culture but also in the inner battlegrounds of our own souls.

Thus the need also for humility. How we speak and act faithfully in the larger public realm while working out our salvation with the requisite fear and trembling (see Philippians 2:12)—this challenge is of supreme importance for evangelicals as we think about the proper rhythms of public discipleship.

Overall, then, it is a good thing that evangelicals have been thinking and acting in recent decades in a manner that takes our public lives more seriously. The Christian gospel does call us to serve as witnesses to, and agents of, the kingdom of Christ in all areas of creaturely existence.

So this is an important time for us to think about and commit to new patterns of "holy worldliness." The call to seek the welfare of the cities in which the Lord has placed us is a real one (see Jeremiah 29:7). Yet we must be ever mindful of the need to wait patiently for the real and lasting solutions to the human condition, which will only be implemented when the angel's trumpet signals that Jesus is ready to make everything new. It is a good thing, I think, that we have learned to sing, "Shine, Jesus, shine, fill this land with the Father's glory." But we should make it a practice regularly to follow that song with a verse of "In the Sweet By and By":

> We shall sing on that beautiful shore
> The melodious songs of the blest;
> And our spirits shall sorrow no more—
> Not a sigh for the blessing of rest.
> In the sweet by and by,
> We shall meet on that beautiful shore;
> In the sweet by and by,
> We shall meet on that beautiful shore.

CHAPTER FIFTEEN

BEYOND COMPLEXITY

et me provide a label for what I have been doing in this book. I have been attempting to promote a "second naivete" for evangelicals. David Hubbard, my presidential predecessor at Fuller Seminary, liked to quote a line from nineteenth-century New English poet Oliver Wendell Holmes: "I do not give a fig for the simplicity that is prior to complexity; but I would give my right arm for the simplicity that lies *beyond* complexity." This remark gets at the kind of thing the French philosopher Paul Ricoeur had in mind when he wrote about "the second naivete."[1]

The first naivete happens when we see things in quite uncomplicated terms—they strike us as simple and straightforward. But then something forces us into a questioning mood, and we subject those ideas to critical examination. Some folks get stuck at this stage—they suspend belief and get caught up in a mood of endless questioning. This isn't healthy, Ricoeur argued. We need to embrace again the beliefs that have held up well under critical scrutiny. However, we can't just forget all the questions we asked and go back to the earlier simplicity. Instead we must move ahead to the *second* naivete.

It should be clear from what I've written in these pages that I have no desire to romanticize the sawdust trail. There are things about the sawdust trail—tendencies that have often manifested themselves as full-blown errors—that I strongly dislike. I am happy Edward John Carnell wrote his candid critique of fundamentalism. His book came into my life at a time when I very much needed to be assured I could go beyond the first naivete without thereby abandoning biblical orthodoxy. But I have also come to discover that the weak points of the sawdust trail are closely related to the strong points. There is very little about the legacy of the gospel tent that I want simply to reject outright. Instead, I find myself sorting things out, reworking, separating good elements from bad ones. In doing so, I find myself moving beyond complexity to a new sense of what is really basic and nonnegotiable. I enter a "second naivete." This is what I want for myself: "the simplicity that lies beyond complexity." This is also what I want for the evangelical movement: a mature rediscovery of what was good about the sawdust trail.

Radical Commitment

A well-known "ecumenical" theologian was addressing a group of pastors on the need for the church to take a new approach to missions in the new millennium. His basic recommendation was that we need to stop trying to evangelize people from other religions and instead engage them in friendly interreligious dialogue. To illustrate his contention that Christian evangelism is an arrogant activity, he told about a time when he was traveling by train with a Hindu friend in an Asian country. They were approached by a teenage boy who insisted on talking to them about his Christian faith. The lad told them that he had only recently "met Christ," but that his life had already been changed in some wonderful ways.

They politely listened to his story and then made it clear they were not interested in an extended conversation.

The theologian told us how offended he was by this encounter. His Hindu friend was a scholar who had devoted a lifetime to his own spiritual pursuits. What right did a teenage boy, newly filled with religious zeal, have to try to instruct such a person on matters of religious significance? Indeed, the theologian asked, what business did a young person like that have going around telling people what it means to "know Jesus"?

I was the next speaker on the program, and I felt obligated to address those questions. I told the group how I as a teenager walked down the aisle to accept Jesus at a Billy Graham evangelistic meeting. I testified to the importance of that encounter for me in my spiritual pilgrimage. In a very public way I was committing my life to Jesus Christ. Looking back, I know I didn't understand all the implications of what I was doing. But, I told the audience, neither did I understand all the implications of what I was doing when I first said "I love you" to the young woman who was to become my wife. But that act was a commitment to a journey that has lasted now for decades. It was the beginning of a life-transforming relationship. And my teenage decision to accept Christ as a personal Savior was also a decision that had profound—and eternal—consequences, even if there was much about it at the time that was immature.

In the mid-1980s Robert Bellah and his associates published *Habits of the Heart,* one of the most widely discussed books about North American culture to appear in recent years. The Bellah team chose this phrase as their subtitle: *Individualism and Commitment in American Life.* In doing so they meant to highlight their conviction that making and sustaining commitments has become a problematic thing in contemporary life. And they were not alone then, and are not alone now, in seeing this as an important issue.

The divorce rate, the weakening of family bonds, the deterioration of patterns of citizenship and civic virtue—all of these are manifestations of a crisis of commitment.

The sawdust trail was a place where people were encouraged to make deep and abiding commitments. And nothing short of putting "your all on the altar" would do. Those of us who sat through those calls to commitment know the ritual well: "Every head bowed, every eye closed. No one looking around, please. The Lord is speaking to your heart. He wants you to decide tonight. Don't put it off. Tell him you want to give him your all. Maybe you have never yielded your life to him ... or maybe you are a Christian but there is something in your life you've been holding back.... He wants your obedience right now. He's Lord of all, or not Lord at all." These strike me today as good and healthy words of pleading. We need to issue and hear these calls to commitment today with a second naivete.

Believing the Bible

There's a story that regularly makes the rounds about a well-known theologian—in most versions it is Karl Barth—who was asked to make a profound theological statement, and he responded with: "Jesus loves me! this I know, for the Bible tells me so." This is a nice "second naivete" tale. You know that the great theologian had spent a lifetime thinking weighty and complex theological thoughts. But when asked to summarize it all, he went back to a simple children's song about a Book from God that tells about a Savior's love.

For many of us the Bible is a much more complex book than it seemed to be when we first heard the stories in Sunday school. This is not only understandable—it is a *good* thing it has gotten more complex for us. But it is also good to remember our *first* naivete, and then to reappropriate that kind of understanding in embracing a simplicity that is beyond complexity.

Wonder

A reporter once called to ask me about life on other planets. He was writing about why people are fascinated with that possibility, and he wanted to include, he said, "the religious angle." He had gotten the impression that the whole notion of extraterrestial life was threatening to evangelicals. Did I feel threatened?

I asked him if he had ever attended a Billy Graham crusade. He had—once. Did he hear them sing, "How Great Thou Art"? I asked. He thought he might have, but he asked me to refresh his memory. I quoted the opening line: "O Lord my God, when I in awesome wonder consider all the worlds thy hands have made." I did not doubt his report that many evangelicals are threatened by the notion of life on other planets—but I did think it odd that these same folks could sing this line of this great hymn without making the connection.

Earlier I reported that I am quite willing these days to live with a little messiness in my theology. I don't think this means I have been too enamored with a "postmodern" willingness to tolerate incoherence. I think it's because I have become much more disposed to appreciate the place of *wonder* in the Christian life. The sawdust trail gave me the categories for expressing this sense of wonder: "Consider all the worlds Thy hands have made."

The wonder of the love of God—a love that "goes beyond the highest star and reaches to the lowest hell." The wonder of the grace of God—"And can it be that I should gain an int'rest in the Savior's blood?... 'Tis mercy all, immense and free, for O, my God, it found out me." The wonder of Jesus, my Redeemer—"I stand amazed in the presence of Jesus the Nazarene, and wonder how He could love me, a sinner condemned, unclean."

Wonder is not a uniquely evangelical experience. We have much to learn from other traditions of wonder. But evangelicals have focused in a special way on the wonder of a divine love that could send the Savior to the cross for the likes of us. People on the sawdust trail wept tears over that kind of love and sang praises to "the love that drew salvation's plan!" I hope evangelicals will continue to shed those tears until Jesus comes to wipe every tear from their eyes forever. And I hope those particular songs of praise will never be forgotten—and that the smell of sawdust will forever linger in the air.

Chapter One: Of Tents and Trails

1. Annie Dillard, "The Book of Luke," *The Annie Dillard Reader* (New York: HarperCollins, 1994), 267.

2. Martin Heidegger, "Letter on Humanism," in Martin Heidegger, *Basic Writings: from Being and Time (1927) to The Task of Thinking (1964)*, ed. David Farrell Krell (New York: Harper & Row, 1977), 239.

3. Kenneth J. Gergen, *The Saturated Self: Dilemmas of Identity in Contemporary Life* (New York: Basic Books, 1991), 256.

Chapter Two: Natural Spirituality

1. Chester P. Michael and Marie C. Norrisey, *Prayer and Temperament: Different Prayer Forms for Different Personality Types*, rev. ed. (Charlottesville, Va.: Open Door, 1991).

2. All quotes in this paragraph come from Abraham Kuyper, *To Be Near Unto God*, translated by John Hendrik DeVries (Grand Rapids: Baker, 1939), 549–52.

Chapter Four: The Making of a Convinced Evangelical

1. Joel A. Carpenter, *Revive Us Again: The Reawakening of American Fundamentalism* (New York: Oxford Univ. Press, 1997), 87.

2. Edward John Carnell, *The Case for Orthodox Theology* (Philadelphia: Westminster, 1959), 120–21.

3. George William Rutler, *Brightest and Best: Stories of Hymns* (San Francisco: Ignatius Press, 1998), 147.

Chapter Five: Mindful Evangelicalism

1. Carl F. H. Henry, *The Uneasy Conscience of Modern Fundamentalism* (Grand Rapids: Eerdmans, 1947), 70.

2. Mark A. Noll, *The Scandal of the Evangelical Mind* (Grand Rapids: Eerdmans, 1994), ix.

3. Alister McGrath, *Evangelicalism and the Future of Christianity* (Downers Grove, Ill.: InterVarsity Press, 1995), 189.

Chapter Six: Fundamentalism Revisited

1. Joel A. Carpenter, *Revive Us Again: The Reawakening of American Fundamentalism* (New York: Oxford Univ. Press, 1997), 87.

2. Carpenter, *Revive Us Again*, 87.

3. Carpenter, *Revive Us Again*, 87.

4. Carpenter, *Revive Us Again*, 88.

5. Carpenter, *Revive Us Again*, 239.

6. Carpenter, *Revive Us Again*, 239.

7. Carpenter, *Revive Us Again*, 240.

8. Imagery taken from Martin Luther's hymn, "A Mighty Fortress Is Our God," stanza 4.

Chapter Eight: To the Jew First

1. The article "Prominent Evangelical Clearly Advocates Proselytizing Jews" by Debra Nussbaum Cohen appears on the Internet at JTA ON LINE [http://jta.virtualjerusalem.com/index.exe?9708126]. The Jewish Telegraphic Agency (JTA) is an international news service that provides up-to-the-minute reports, analysis pieces, and features on events and issues of concern to the Jewish people.

2. Lewis Sperry Chafer, *Dispensationalism* (Dallas: Dallas Sem. Press, 1936), 41.

3. Corrie ten Boom, with John and Elizabeth Sherrill, *The Hiding Place* (Washington Depot, Conn.: Chosen, 1971), 68.

Chapter Ten: Understanding Sister Helen's Tears

1. Quoted in David B. Calhoun, *Princeton Seminary: Faith & Learning, 1812–1868*, vol. 1 (Carlisle, Penn.: The Banner of Truth, 1994), 305.

2. Quoted in Calhoun, *Princeton Seminary: Faith & Learning, 1812–1868*, vol. 1, 305.

3. Discussed and quoted in Lyle W. Dorsett, *A Passion for Souls: The Life of D. L. Moody* (Chicago: Moody Press, 1997), 238–40.

Chapter Eleven: "Real" Evangelism

1. Paul Tillich, *The Shaking of the Foundations* (New York: Charles Scribner's Sons, 1948), 145.

2. Sandra S. Sizer, *Gospel Hymns and Social Religion: The Rhetoric of Nineteenth-Century Revivalism* (Philadelphia: Temple Univ. Press, 1978).

Chapter Thirteen: A Word Hidden in the Heart

1. Annie Dillard, "The Book of Luke," *The Annie Dillard Reader* (New York: HarperCollins, 1994), 267.

2. Dillard, "The Book of Luke," *The Annie Dillard Reader*, 268.

Chapter Fifteen: Beyond Complexity

1. Paul Ricoeur, *The Symbolism of Evil* (New York: Harper & Row, 1967), 349.

We want to hear from you. Please send your comments about this
book to us in care of the address below. Thank you.

ZondervanPublishingHouse
Grand Rapids, Michigan 49530
http://www.zondervan.com